READING MATTER

READING MATTER

Multidisciplinary Perspectives on Material Culture

Arthur Asa Berger

Transaction Publishers
New Brunswick (U.S.A.) and London (U.K.)

Library of Congress Catalog Number: 91-8384
ISBN: 0-88738-435-8
Printed in the United States of America

Library of Congress Cataloging-in-Publication Data

Berger, Arthur Asa, 1933–
    Reading matter : multi-disciplinary perspectives on material
culture / Arthur Asa Berger.
        p.   cm.
    Includes bibliographical references (p.) and index.
    ISBN 0-88738-435-8
    1. Material culture.   2. Popular culture.   3. Fads.   4. Jeans
(Clothing)   I. Title.
GN406.B47 1991
306.4 – dc20   91-8384
                                                       CIP

To say that Omo *cleans in depth (see the Cinema Publicite advertisement) is to assume that linen is deep, which no one had previously thought, and this unquestionably results in exalting it, by establishing it as an object favoura- ble to those obscure tendencies to enfold and caress which are found in every human body. As for foam, it is well known that it signifies luxury. To begin with, it appears to lack any usefulness; then, its abundant, easy, almost infinite proliferation allows one to suppose there is in the substance from which it issues a vigorous germ, a healthy and powerful essence, a great wealth of active ingredients in a small original volume. Finally, it gratifies in the consumer a tendency to imagine matter as something airy, with which contact is effected in a mode both light and vertical. . . .*

— Roland Barthes, *Mythologies*

Contents

.

Consider, for example, the Washlet, a technological wonder that takes the guesswork out of cleaning up. A kind of toilet bowl-cum-bidet, the Washlet sprays a water jet, then dries with a blast of of warm air. For added comfort, the seat is heated. It even has a safety device: to prevent the mechanically inquisitive from being sprayed in the face, the water nozzle will not work unless a sensor registers the presence of a seat upon the seat. The fruit of a two-year survey of the Japanese anatomy — in search of the perfect angle for the water nozzle — the Washlet is being aggressively marketed by its manufacturer, TOTO, Japan's largest maker of toilets. Promise the ads: "Your bottom will like it after three tries."

—Michael Walsh, *Time*, 13 February 1989

Preface

Please imagine the following. Six scholars (all eminent researchers) have offices in a circular building surrounding a small courtyard. The heroes and heroines of this little adventure are a semiotician, a psychoanalytic psychologist, an anthropologist, an historian, a sociologist, and a Marxist political scientist. In actuality, one researcher might use a number of these disciplines, techniques, modes of inquiry — or whatever you might wish to call them — at the same time. There are, for example, sociologists and anthropologists who are also Marxists and, in addition, use psychoanalytic and semiotic modes of analysis in their work.

In the center of this circular courtyard, on a table, is a McDonald's hamburger, a package of French fries, and a milkshake. Each of our researchers looks out of the window of his or her office and sees the hamburger, French fries, and milkshake, from a slightly different perspective, and speculates about what the hamburger reveals or reflects about American society and culture.

The semiotician sees McDonald's as a symbol of Americanness, of our efficiency, of our modernity (or is it now postmodernity?), of our ability to fuse the techniques of mass production and cooking hamburgers in the interest of speed, of standardization, and of our throwaway culture. Along with Coca-Cola, the McDonald's hamburger is probably the most commonly known symbol of American culture.

The psychoanalyst sees in the McDonald phenomenon the need for instant gratification, the desire for community (with all the other McDonald's hamburger eaters) and, at the same time, an element of depersonalization and dehumanization. One has little choice in how the hamburger will be cooked. They are cooked on an assembly line in prodigious quantities. Ironically, McDonald's commercials stress (or used to stress) individuality and choice in campaigns such as "You, you're the one" and "We do it all for you." Many of the commercials, especially those in the recent past, had a good deal of quick cutting in them which generated a lot of visual excitement. This visual excitement carried over in many people's minds, it has been suggested, into the actual matter of going to McDonald's — which was seen as an "exciting" experience.

The anthropologist focuses on the ritualistic and highly structured aspects of the McDonald's experience and of the way McDonald's has become part of American folklore. The arches also might be seen to have a religious significance and the whole phenomenon as having the same dynamics of American evangelical religions. McDonald's now are found all over the world. A recent McDonald's commercial about the McDonald's restaurant in Moscow (which serves 30,000 hamburgers a day) shows the faces of Russian McDonald's patrons with expressions that can best be described as ecstatic. The expressions on people's faces are remarkably similar to those of believers are religious shrines.

An historian would be interested in the evolution of the McDonald's corporation, from rather humble beginnings to a position now in which something like seven percent of all restaurant meals in America are eaten in McDonald's. Our historian might also investigate the role McDonald's, as a powerful corporation, has played in American political life and society and how McDonald's restaurants have changed and evolved over the years.

The sociological approach would consider the part McDonald's plays in American youth culture and of McDonald's use, and some would say exploitation, of young people (and now senior citizens) in its restaurants. McDonald's (and other fast food chains) are having trouble recruiting American young people now, so the jobs are going to minority youths and new immigrants. It is not "cool" to work at McDonald's according to many American youngsters. (The role McDonald's plays in training potentially dysfunctional people to participate effectively in the work force might also be investigated. Many of these people come from disadvantaged families or from abroad and do not have the American work ethic.) McDonald's could also be studied in terms of the whole fast food industry and the decline of the family meal in many American families.

A Marxist interpretation of the McDonald's phenomenon would focus on the exploitation of the young and old workers, who, until recently, worked for little more than the minimum wage. McDonald's might be seen as an example of mystification—equal access to McDonald's, which are relatively inexpensive, is interpreted by many people to show that we live in a "more or less" classless society in which the good things in life, like McDonald's hamburgers, are available to all. (The wealthy classes, of course, eat steak or hamburgers cooked to order while the poor eat mass-produced cheapie hamburgers to satisfy their craving for meat.) Until July 1990, McDonald's cooked its French fries in a combination of vegetable oil and beef tallow. This was done to maximize profits, at the expense of the health of the patrons. It was only after an expensive campaign was waged that McDonald's agreed to get rid of the beef tallow. But this may be too late for millions and millions of young people with plugged up arteries, arteries (according to some studies) similar to those found in people more than fifty years of age.

There could, of course, be other scholars with offices in the complex, who would have other perspectives on the "meanings" of a McDonald's hamburger and the McDonald's corporation (and by extension fast food joints in general). Nutritionists, business professors, feminist writers, advertising professors, architects, graphic designers, and many others would have valuable insights to offer and interesting things to say about this phenomenon.

In the 26 July 1990 *New York Times* there was an article by Joan Kron about a cultural anthropologist, Grant McCracken, who studies "Homeyness" in people. Kron points out that McCracken spent a decade studying how "meaning is 'manufactured' and attached to goods, and how consumers make the meanings their own" (1990, B5). Shopping, then, becomes, McCracken suggests, "a much more systematic and sensible activity than most people think" since it is, in reality, "a cultural project to complete the self" (1990, B5). "We depend on objects for their meanings," he adds, "and then disavow their significance at every turn."

The article also deals with the difficulties McCracken has had getting his work published because mainstream academia sees his interest in "homeyness" and artifacts as "trivial." This article is interesting on two accounts. First, it shows that people don't wish to attribute significance to the objects they surround themselves with (is this some kind of repression?) and second, studying the material culture of contemporary or complex societies has its perils. Doing the same for a preliterate society causes no problems, I might add. It is standard anthropological procedure.

One reason analyzing material culture is so problematical for many academicians (and others) is that it is a multidisciplinary kind of research and we still haven't figured out very well how to do this kind of research. Auden wrote "each in the prison of his self is convinced of his own freedom." We might amend that to read "each in the prison of his own discipline is convinced of its own centrality." This is not an unusual situation. A neurologist friend of mine told me that many neurologists consider medicine to be a subdiscipline of neurology.

Let me offer here a list of things I have done or tried to do when analyzing material culture, despite the professional difficulties that are often connected with this fascinating and dangerous enterprise.

1. *Different artifacts require different approaches.* You have to determine which combination of approaches offers the most valuable insights into the meaning and function of the artifact. Some artifacts, such as the McDonald's hamburger, open themselves to many different approaches, but others do not.

2. *Specific concepts must be used in interpreting artifacts.* It is easy to deal in generalities when writing about artifacts, but these generalities are not enough. One must, to the extent it is possible, find concepts within a given discipline that help us find meaning in the artifact. A good example of this can be found in the chapter on psychoanalytic approaches, in which certain artifacts have, I suggest, id or ego or superego significance. I would argue, for instance, that a bikini is essentially an "id" garment. I don't think this is terribly farfetched or

that the notion of interpreting garments or other objects and artifacts in terms of Freud's trichotomy is too hard to swallow.

3. *The more you know the more you see.* You need to know a great deal about a number of complicated things to make sense of "simple" things. It was Marshall McLuhan's wide-ranging knowledge that enabled him to interpret in such perceptive and meaningful ways the various artifacts and example of media he analyzed in *The Mechanical Bride*.

4. *You must avoid being doctrinaire and imposing your categories or concepts on an artifact.* We are dealing here with a basic criticism one always hears when interpreting anything. People often accuse me, and others like me, of "reading things into" artifacts and objects, things "that aren't there." If a person doesn't accept Freud's notion of the unconscious and of the id, ego, and superego or of oral, anal, phallic, and genital stages of sexual development, then of course we will be accused of reading things in when we make an analysis. Our methodology is not accepted and that ends the argument. But even if people do accept such concepts, they often find it difficult to make the connection between the concept and the application of the concept to the artifact in question. My suggestion is that one has to make as strong an argument as one can and let things go at that.

There's no way of "compelling" people to accept interpretations we make. We analysts also might retain a certain amount of humility, for it may be, in some cases, that we are not making correct or the best interpretations of our artifacts. The other side of this problem is that there are people who don't see enough in artifacts and material culture. They are "blind" to the meanings these things have, for a variety of reasons.

5. *Don't let the quantitative analysts get you down.* Some scholars consider any research that is not quantitative to be basically a matter of mere "opinion" and not worth serious consideration. They like numbers and find security in them. But even numbers have to be interpreted, and the same numbers are often interpreted in strikingly dissimilar ways. ("Figures don't lie," as the saying goes, "but liars figure.") This is often the case in economics, probably the most quantitative of our social sciences. Economists use quantitative data or numbers to make arguments that ultimately have to be evaluated on their logic and face value; in this respect they are no different from researchers who use qualitative methods. Analyzing material culture is an important enterprise and a useful way to gain insights into everyday life, the objects and activities which form the basis of our lives and which seem so trivial because they occupy so much of our lives. We must ponder what Malinowski called "the imponderabilia" of everyday life and mine it for the gold that is buried in it.

Artifacts and useful objects are a part of all recorded history. They are devised, invented, and made as adjuncts to the human being's ability to accomplish work or enjoy pleasure. A close examination of any object is a graphic description of the level of intelligence, manual dexterity, and artistic comprehension of the civilization that produced it. It can reflect, as well, the climate, religious beliefs, form of government, the natural materials at hand, the structure of commerce, and the extent of man's scientific and emotional sophistication.

All of these observations are read out of a simple artifact by a skilled archaeologist with or without benefit of the written word. All of these things are read out of objects every day by the unskilled layman. It is the silent language of the senses. It occurs at the unspoken, emotional level, and judgments are formed, trains of logic instigated, and action taken on the basis of this language.

—Richard S. Latham,
"The Artifact as a Cultural Cipher"

Introduction

To be civilized, whatever else it may be, involves making, using and buying objects. We started with stone tools and have moved on, rather quickly (relatively speaking) to computers and rocket ships. These objects play an important role in our lives. As Ernest Dichter, the "father" of motivational research writes in *The Strategy of Desire* (1960,91):

> The objects which surround us do not simply have utilitarian aspects; rather they serve as a kind of mirror which reflects our own image. Objects which surround us permit us to discover more and more aspects of ourselves. . . . In a sense, therefore, the knowledge of the soul of things is possibly a direct and new and revolutionary way of discovering the soul of man.

When Dichter uses the term "soul" he is not using it theologically but psychoanalytically — objects enable us to gain insights into human personality and the human psyche and, by extension, the societies and cultures in which the objects were created.

We use objects because they communicate their messages to us directly, without the filter of language and everything connected with it. I assume, of course, that analyzing material culture, learning to "read" matter, provides us with information and insights different from those that are generated by language and speech, where the element of intention and impression management must be considered.

Many of us have speculated from time to time about the significance of various objects and artifacts (a neighbor's car, a new kitchen appliance, etc.). But generally speaking, this speculation is rather casual. There are, however, people who analyze these objects in systematic ways—anthropologists, historians, semioticians, Marxists, sociologists, and psychologists (among others) in an attempt to elicit from these objects and material culture in general reliable information about people, societies, and cultures.

Let us look at the two words as they are used in scholarly discourse. The term "material" comes from the Latin *materia*, matter. Material suggests an object, something that has a physical nature, that can be seen and touched. Objects have shape and size and color and weight. The objects we are interested in are artifacts, objects which involve human workmanship; after all, a rock is material but it isn't an artifact. We use the term material here to contrast it with a different aspect of human culture, ideas and beliefs and related considerations. Material culture can be defined to cover everything from a pot to a city; my focus in this book will be on relatively simple objects and artifacts—what might be described as small-scale material culture.

Let me distinguish between material culture and nonmaterial or "ideational" culture in the chart that follows:

Material	*Ideational*
objects, artifacts	ideas, beliefs
physical, tangible	mental, cognitive
everyday life	intellectual activity

This lists suggests some important differences between these two realms.

The second term, "culture," is enormously complicated. There are, conservatively speaking, hundreds of definitions of culture. Let me offer a useful one. In Henry Pratt Fairchild's *Dictionary of Sociology and Related Sciences* (1967,80) culture is defined as follows:

A collective name for all behavior patterns socially acquired and transmitted by means of symbols; hence a name for all the distinctive achievements of human groups, including not only such items as language, tool-making, industry, art, science, law, government, morals and religion, but also the material instruments or artifacts in which cultural achievements are embodied and by which intellectual cultural features are given practical effect, such as buildings, tools, machines, communication devices, art objects. etc.

Fairchild points out that culture is symbolic and transmitted and that "intellectual cultural features" are embodied in artifacts—that is, material culture.

We analyze material culture, I suggest, because we believe it offers us unique and valuable insights into people and society. The problem is learning how to analyze material culture in a systematic and reasoned matter. That is the subject of this book. *Reading Matter* discusses a number of methodological approaches that can be used to analyze and interpret material culture and relate it to personality, society, and culture. It assumes that material culture is symbolic and thus has "meaning" that can be elicited.

This is a methods book in which I offer an introduction to the most important concepts in a number of methodologies that can be used to analyze material culture and offer some examples of the ways the concepts can or have been used.

There is a field of study, archaeological anthropology, that studies prehistoric cultures by interpreting the remains they have left (material culture, in essence). These scholars make inferences about these cultures based on these remains and their knowledge of ethnological theory. Archaelogists study everything from fossilized feces (coprolite), bones, and ancient artifacts to the designs of prehistoric settlements. From their work they are able to make inferences about social, economic, and political activities that took place in the settlements they study.

We are concerned here with material culture in relatively recent times (since we've become literate and started recording history) and the present day, however, and our field of research might be thought of as the archaelogy of postliterate societies and cultures. That means we can make use of information we have from historians, economists, sociologists, anthropologists, psychologists, journalists, and travelers when we make our analyses.

We can also study material culture in the past (for example, in the Victorian period in England) and we can compare artifacts from the past with those we have in the present to see how they have evolved. In addition we can see compare American artifacts, of a given time period, with those from other cultures and see how artifacts "diffuse" or spread from one culture to others (think, for example, of Coca-Cola or McDonald's Hamburgers). We use the comparative approach because it is only through comparisons that we are able to make sense of things. I will say more on this subject shortly.

Guidelines to Consider

Material culture is a very large subject. How do we come to grips with it without doing violence to it? Let me suggest some considerations that will help with this matter.

1. *General Categories.* We can focus our attention on certain kinds of material culture or categories of material culture, some of which are listed below:

Foods	Clothing	Furniture	Housing
Buildings	Tools	Health Aids	Weapons
Beauty Aids	Machines	Gadgets	Publications
Vehicles	Pet Supplies	Appliances	Cooking Utensils

For our purposes it makes sense to focus on relatively simple objects or artifacts. Vehicles, for example, are complex collections of artifacts and could easily be the subject of a large book. The same applies to buildings.

2. *Locations of Objects.* Here we consider where we find objects and use that as the organizing logic of any extended analysis we might wish to make. Some of the more significant locations are home, the workplace, stores (supermarkets, department stories, hypermarkets, malls), and institutions (universities, hospitals, museums, government offices). Each of these places is the locus for many different artifacts. For anyone interested in an in-depth exploration of contemporary American material culture, what better source could there be than a Sears' or Ward's catalogue?

It is important to think about where various objects are found in typical households. Are they used for "display" or "public" functions and located in living rooms, dining rooms, or kitchens (where they can be seen by all) or are they used for "private" functions and found in bathrooms or bedrooms? For example, think of the difference between a television set or stereo and a vibrator.

We might also consider the sites where the objects are found in a more general way (cities, regions, nations, etc.) and relate these sites to social, cultural, and historical considerations. Thus, we might deal with the relationships that exist (or may have existed) between these objects and socioeconomic classes and political entities of one sort or another.

3. *Complexity Scale*. Material culture ranges in complexity from simple objects, made of one part (such as a plastic spoon or a piece of paper) to artifacts made of several parts or many parts (such as toaster or a hammer) to machines and, ultimately, to something as complicated as a modern skyscraper or hospital, which probably is as complex an example or locus of material culture as one can get.

4. *Aesthetic Considerations*. Every artifact, by definition, shows human workmanship. This means that there is an aesthetic dimension to material culture, a dimension that is of considerable importance. In analyzing an artifact from an aesthetic perspective we deal with some or all of the following considerations:

a. What is the size of the object and how does the size relate to its impact on people?

b. What is the shape of the object? Is the shape pleasing or unpleasing? Is it bulky? Is it small?

c. What colors are used in the object? How do these colors relate to our sense of style, design, taste, and class?

d. What do you think of the design of the object? Is it streamlined? Does its form "follow" its function? Does the object suggest class and sophistication or cheapness and commonness? How does the design achieve its effects?

e. What materials are used in the object? Are they expensive or common? Are they functional or mostly decorative?

f. What "style" does the object have? How does this style relate to other objects that have the same use or function? Is the object attractive or beautiful in any way? Is there, somehow, an erotic aspect to the object (either in its form, functioning, look)? Is it *kitsch* (that is, defined by certain critics as exceedingly vulgar and "in poor taste") or is it "sophisticated" (whatever that means)?

We should not underestimate the aesthetic appeal of artifacts. I once met a woman who had something like a hundred pair of shoes and occasionally even bought a pair of shoes that didn't fit her (because she felt they were so beautiful). And of course there is the celebrated case of Imelda Marcos, who had several thousand pairs of shoes. This affliction (or fixation) is not typical of most women (or men) but it shows the power of aesthetic factors in our decision-making. We are not always completely rational when it comes to purchasing shoes and many other objects, as well.

5. *Functions of Objects.* Here we investigate the role artifacts play in our individual lives and in society in general. Are some objects the functional equivalent of other objects? Do certain objects replace other objects? If so, why and what significance does this have? Are some objects so important (think of the microwave oven here) that they have an enormous impact on life in general? If so, why do they assume this role and what do they tell us about the societies and cultures in which they are found? And how do objects relate to such considerations as gender, race, ethnicity, socioeconomic class, and education?

Methods of Reading Matter

I will offer discussions of some of the main concepts found in semiotic analysis, historical analysis, anthropological analysis, psychoanalytic analysis, Marxist analysis, and sociological analysis. These methods often overlap, as I pointed our earlier, so it is not unusual to find historians using psychoanalytic and semiotic concepts in their work.

In this book you will find discussions and interpretations of the following topics: Barbie Dolls, matches, furniture, cigarette lighters, toys, Pachinko, Coca-Cola bottles, McDonald's hamburgers, male clothing, men's underwear, bread, steak dinners, video games, clocks, Charlie McCarthy, computers, microwave ovens, and matzoh. And, as they say, "much, much more."

The second portion of the book uses these disciplines to investigate one subject—fashion and an important aspect of fashion, blue jeans and what I call the "denimization" phenomenon. This section shows how different methods of "reading" material culture end up with different perspectives on things—even when they are dealing with the same topic.

And now, let us begin with a discussion of semiotic analysis. I have started with semiotics because it can be argued that all the approaches used in this book are, in part, semiotic and as some semioticians would argue, all disciplines are implicitly when they are not explicitly semiotic in a universe, as Peirce put it, "perfused" with signs if not made up entirely of signs.

Part I

Analyzing Material Culture

From the perspective of this analysis lox differs from all other preserved fish preparations in one way: It is as red as blood. The glossy redness of the fish, in combination with the opaque whiteness of the cheese, results in a striking contrast. Indeed, children frequently refuse to eat lox because of its visual resemblance to raw meat. The coming together of these two foods produces a visual pun. Although a permitted combination, lox and cream cheese give the appearance of violating the strong taboo on mixing milkhik *and* fleishik.

This suggestion can be supported from another direction since in many other cultures the ritual use of white and red refers to male and female, respectively. The reference to semen and menstrual blood, often perceived as two elements required for conception in folk biology, lies just beneath the surface of this symbolic opposition. Indeed, this idea is made almost explicit in the Talmud: "The white substance . . . is supplied by the man, from whom comes the child's brain, bones and sinews; the red substance . . . is supplied by the woman from whom comes its skin, flesh, and blood.

—Stanley Regelson,
"The Bagel: Symbol and Ritual at the Breakfast Table"

1

Semiotic Analysis of Material Culture

The goal of semiotics is to discover how meaning is conveyed and generated by texts (films, television shows, literary works) and, for our purposes, by objects, artifacts, and material culture in general. (In this book, material culture will be understood to mean nonverbal aspects of culture, objects showing human workmanship — which is the conventional definition of an artifact.) Semiotics has a long history, but modern semiotics is generally held to have been founded by two thinkers — the Swiss linguist Ferdinand de Saussure (1857–1913) and the American philosopher Charles Sanders Peirce (1839–1914). Semiotics is an extremely complicated and often very technical subject, but it is possible, by learning the fundamental principles of semiotics, to analyze material culture in interesting and suggestive ways.

The fundamental concept of semiotics is that of the sign, which can be defined, generally speaking, as anything that can be used to represent or stand for something else. As Umberto Eco writes in *A Theory of Signs* (1976,7), "A sign is everything which can be taken as significantly substituting for something else."

For Saussure, a sign is composed of two parts — a signifier (sound-image) and a signified (concept). The relationship that exists between a signifier and signified is arbitrary or a matter of convention.

Words are an important kind of sign. In English, we use the word (signifier) "tree" to stand for a certain kind of object (signified) — a woody perennial plant having a long main stem and relatively few branches. There is no "natural" connection between the word we use for this object and the object itself, and in other countries, where different languages are spoken, there are different words used for the same object. Thus Saussure writes (1966, 67):

> The bond between the signifier and the signified is arbitrary. Since I mean by sign the whole that results from the associating of the signifier with the signified, I can simply say *the linguistic sign is arbitrary*.

This notion of the arbitrary or, more precisely, conventional relationship between a signifier and signified is one of the cornerstones of Saussure's thought. The only exception to this involves symbols, which Saussure suggested involved signifiers and signifieds that were not completely arbitrary. As an example, Saussure mentions a common symbol of justice, a pair of scales that, he says, cannot be replaced "with just any other symbol, such as a chariot."

From the Saussurean perspective, we can look upon objects and artifacts as signs, and, in particular, signifiers. If the artifact is the signifier, what, we must ask, is being signified? To answer that, let us turn to another important notion we get from Saussure, which is that concepts (ideas used to explain phenomena) can only be understood differentially.

Concepts only have meaning, Saussure argued, by differing from other concepts. That is, meaning doesn't stem from some kind of an essence or "content" a concept has but from the relationships that exist between that concept and other concepts. As Saussure wrote (1966,117):

> Concepts are purely differential and defined not by their positive content but negatively by their relations with the other terms of the system. Their most precise characteristic is in being what the others are not.

This is a very important notion, for it forces us to look at objects in terms of their relations to other objects and the system or systems of objects that exist in a given society. Nothing has meaning in itself and relationships are all important.

The most important relationship we find tends to involve opposition, which is not the same thing as negation. There is a difference between rich and unrich (the negation) and rich and poor (the opposition). The reason oppositions are so important is that using them seems to be the way the mind works. As Jonathan Culler has written (1976,15):

> Structuralists have generally followed Jakobson and taken the binary opposition as a fundamental operation of the human mind basic to the production of meaning.

This is not the same thing as saying there are only two sides to an argument or that everything must be seen in terms of black and white.

Let me offer a list of a number of oppositions that might be of use in analyzing material culture:

Electronic	Mechanical
Bright	Dull
Stylish	Common
Modern	Classical
Expensive	Cheap
Handcrafted	Mass Produced
Functional	Useless
Digital	Analog

When we analyze artifacts we do a number of things at the same time: we evaluate them according to various canons of taste and propriety, we connect them to important values and belief systems and we relate them to the stage of technology and the economy and political institutions of the society creating them.

Peirce was also interested in signs, but he developed a different approach to analyzing them. He said there were three kinds of signs—icons, indexes and symbols—which are explained in Table 1.1.

TABLE 1.1 Three Aspects of Signs

SIGN TYPE	ICON	INDEX	SYMBOL
SIGNIFY BY	Resemblance	Causal connections	Convention
EXAMPLES	Photograph	Smoke/Fire	Words
	Pictures	Symptom/Disease	Flags
PROCESS	Can see	Can figure out	Must learn

Source: Berger 1982, 15.

Icons signify by resemblance, indexical signs signify by causal connections (which have to be inferred) and symbols signify by convention (which means we must learn what symbols mean).

As Peirce has written (quoted in J. Jay Zeman, "Peirce's Theory of Signs" in T. Sebeok, *A Perfusion of Signs*, 1977,36):

> . . . every sign is determined by its object, either first, by partaking in the characters of the object, when I call the sign an *Icon*; secondly, by being really and in its individual existence connected with the individual object, when I call the sign an *Index*; thirdly, by more or less approximate certainty that it will be interpreted as denoting the object, in consequence of a habit (which term I use as including a natural disposition), when I call the sign a *Symbol*."

For our particular purposes it is the indexicality of signs that is of most concern. Let me offer an analogy here, involving medicine.

Physicians must interpret signs (which are physical manifestations) and symptoms (which are linguistic) indexically and try to determine what illnesses or problems they represent. This is done by interpreting the signs and symptoms in the context of a knowledge of human physiology and related concerns. Analysts of material culture must function in a similar way and interpret a given artifact with reference to the society and culture in whic it is found.

How does the object reflect the society in which it is found? What, if anything, does the object tell us about the level of technological development of the society and the economic and social and political institutions found in it?

Semiotics is an "imperialistic" science (or, if you don't wish to grant it the status of being a science, an "imperialist" methodology) which has implications for every area of knowledge. Peirce said, "The universe is perfused with signs, if not made entirely of them." That means there's plenty to do for semioticians, and, in particular, for those analysts of material culture who wish to use semiotic techniques. Eco has suggested that analyzing objects is one of the main concerns of semiotics. In the introduction to *A Theory of Semiotics* he lists "Systems of Objects" and writes that "objects as communicative devices come within the realm of semiotics, ranging from architecture to objects in general" (1976,12). Let me now turn to a number of examples of semiotics "in action" and, especially, as semiotics has been used to analyze material culture.

Anyone familiar with the Sherlock Holmes books, films, or television programs knows that at a certain moment, after Holmes has solved some extremely difficult mystery, Watson turns to him and says "By jove, Holmes. How did you do it?" And Holmes replies nonchalantly, "Elementary, my dear Watson." What has Holmes done? Generally speaking, he applies semiotic analysis (without, of course, being aware that this science or methodology exists) to various objects and events and, on the basis of his interpretations of various signs, astounds everyone.

In "The Blue Carbuncle," he gives a large hat to Watson and asks him to tell what kind of a person wore it. Watson, looking the hat over, tells him "I see nothing." "On the contrary, Watson, you can see everything. *You fail, however, to reason from what you see. You are too timid in drawing your inferences,*" [my italics] replies Holmes. Then, on the basis of various signifiers (the size of the hat, the fact that some hair was stuck on the lining, that the hatband was silk and discolored, that the hat was dusty and cracked and spotted in several places, etc.) Holmes proceeds to describe the owner in great detail, even explaining that the man's wife has probably ceased to love him and that they have no gas in their household.

What Holmes has done is use every signifier he could find by observing the hat carefully to infer, using logic and a great deal of information about human physiology and personality, what the man who owned the hat was probably like. In that respect Holmes is a model for us and we might consider analyzing material culture to be, in certain respects, like detective work. We must be careful, of course, about being too bold (not too timid) in drawing our inferences. (For a more elaborate discussion of Holmes as a semiotican, see Berger 1989, 16–18.)

Roland Barthes, the famous French scholar, wrote numerous books on everything from semiological theory to the analysis of narrativity. One of his most famous books, *Mythologies*, contains almost thirty short essays that deal with various aspects of French mass culture and a long theoretical (and ideological) essay on myth and its relation to society. Barthes writes about everything from wrestling and Garbo's face to soap powder and toys.

In his semiotic analysis of French toys, Barthes makes a number of interesting points about the ways these toys reflect French culture and society. I have quoted him, when possible, to show the flavor of his prose, which is very distinctive (Barthes 1972,53,54):

1. "The adult Frenchman sees the child as another self." They are seen as a "smaller" man, and not as radically different from adults.

2. "French toys *always mean something*, and this something is always entirely socialized, consituted by the myths or the techniques of modern adult life: the Army, Broadcasting, the Post Office, Medicine . . . School, Hair-Styling . . . the Air Force."

3. "Toys here reveal the list of all the things the adult does not find unusual: war, bureaucracy, ugliness, Martians, etc."

4. "Dolls which urinate . . . [are] meant to prepare the little girl for the causality of house-keeping, to 'condition' her for her future role as a mother."

5. "The child can only identify himself as owner, as user, never as creator; he does not invent the world, he uses it: there are, prepared for him, actions without adventure, without wonder, without joy . . . he is never allowed to discover anything from start to finish."

6. "French toys are usually based on imitation, they are meant to produce children who are users, not creators."

7. "The bourgeois status of toys can be recognized not only in their forms, which are all functional, but in their substances. Current toys are made of a graceless material, the product of chemistry, not of nature . . . the plastic material of which they are made has an appear-

ance at once gross and hygienic, it destroys all the pleasure, the sweetness, the humanity of touch." Barthes contrasts plastic with wood, which he thinks is much better for children, since it has a natural warmth. "Wood makes essential objects, objects for all time," he writes.

What Barthes has done is to analyze toys (in terms of their functions, nature, physical makeup) as signs and use his knowledge of French history, literature, politics, and culture as a means of interpreting these signs.

He did something quite different with Japan, writing a book, *Empire of Signs*, which was similar in nature to *Mythologies*, but about a culture that was very strange to him. In *Empire of Signs* he writes about various aspects of material culture: Japanese dinner trays, clear soups, chopsticks, sukiyaki, pachinko, packages and the dolls used in Bunraku theatre, for example.

His analysis of pachinko is typical of the essays in the book. In his essay he contrasts Western pinball machines and Japanese pachinko as follows (1982,28–29):

> The Western machine sustains a symbolism of penetration: the point is to possess, by a well-placed thrust, the pinup girl who, all lit up on the panel of the machines, allures and waits. In pachinko, no sex (in Japan . . . sexuality is in sex, not elsewhere; in the United States, it is the contrary: sex is everywhere, except in sexuality). The machines are mangers, lined up in rows; the player, with an abrupt gesture, renewed so rapidly that it seems uninterrupted, feeds the machine with his metal marbles; he stuffs them in, the way you would stuff a goose; from time to time the machine, filled to capacity, releases its diarrhea of marbles; for a few yen, the player is symbolically spattered with money. Here we understand the seriousness of the game which counters the constipated parsimony of salaries, the constriction of capitalist wealth, with the voluptuous debacle of silver balls, which, all of a sudden, fill the player's hand.

This passage is interesting both in terms of its analysis of the cultural significance of pinball and pachinko and for its stylistic exuberance (resplendent with biological metaphors).

It is quite obvious that Barthes is an impressionistic analyst of material culture, but the semiotic analysis of material culture, as has been mentioned before, is an interpretive technique. Some semioticians are more explicit in connecting their readings of material culture with work by social scientists on related concerns.

Craig Gilborn, who was for a number of years on the staff of the Winterthur Museum, has written an essay, "Pop Iconology: Looking at the Coke Bottle," (Fishwick and Browne 1970) which suggests how one might systematically study artifacts:

> Objects are capable of yielding a considerable amount of information about themselves and the conditions in which they were formed or fashioned. Scholars and scientists in fields such as art history and criticism, archeology, paleontology, and the life and earth sciences use terms and methodologies appropriate to their respective problems of studying primary, non-verbal data.

He suggests that analysts of artifacts use three operations: description, classification, and interpretation. Different disciplines, he adds, focus on one or the other of these operations.

In the description phase, taking Coca-Cola bottles as our subject, one must consider such matters as the ornamental design used in designing these bottles. In the classificatory phase, we segregate "objects on the basis of dissimilar attributes." We want to see, for example, how the Coca-Cola bottle evolved and changed over the years. Finally, we come to the interpretive operation, which asks (1970,21) "*What possible meanings can be derived from the product of our labors?*" Here, there is (1970, 21) "an opportunity and a responsibility for the informed imagination to depart, if necessary, from facts to levels of generalization that may not be entirely supported by the evidence at hand."

Gilborn is rather cautious when it comes to interpeting the Coca-Cola bottle. When he wrote this essay, in 1970, it was, he argued, "the most widely recognized commercial product in the world" (1970, 24) and it is a product that is participatory, cutting across all kinds of social and class distinctions. He has moved here from analyzing the bottle to the product itself.

In an essay in the same book, "Soft Drinks and Hard Ikons," I have suggested that one appeal of the Coke bottle is that it looks vaguely like a woman's breast and that Coke is a second-rate narcotic (a cousin to cocaine) and anesthetic and functions as a luxury item with which people can reward themselves. In its diet formulation, Coke (and other diet soft drinks) represented, I suggested, a desire for "pleasure without consequences" and, as such, was a repudiation of American Puritanism. As such, Diet Coke was, perhaps, the hallmark of a new American society.

It is interesting to note that this essay, written in 1970, dealt with two themes that have become increasingly significant in American culture in recent years: the problem of drugs and the matter of "new American" personality types evolving.

Let me conclude with a passage from Edmund Leach's *Culture and Communication: The Logic by Which Symbols are Connected*. In this book, which introduces structural analysis to social anthropology, Leach argues that things are connected to one another in societies. As he puts it (1976,10):

> I shall assume that *all* the various non-verbal dimensions of culture, such as styles in clothing, village lay-out, architecture, furniture, food, cooking, music, physical gestures, postural attitudes and so on are organized in patterned sets so as to incorporate coded information in a manner analagous to the sounds and words and sentences of a natural language. I assume therefore it is just as meaningful to talk about the grammatical rules which govern the wearing of clothes as it is to talk about the grammatical rules which govern speech utterances.

Artifacts do not just exist alone, isolated and unrelated to other aspects of a culture. That means we can use artifacts to discover interesting things about culture and we can use culture to help interpret artifacts.

We are, in a sense, back where we started — with Saussure, who argued in *Course in General Linguistics* that language is a system of signs and that a science which studied the "the life of signs in society" was possible. It is important to remember that Saussure stressed the important roles that signs play in society. There is a social dimension to the enterprise. Using the fundamental principles of semiology and semiotics we can find how artifacts generate meaning and discern the way they function in our lives and our societies.

Art history has defined its data and perceived relationships between these data (arts and artifacts) and society (history) in three ways: by an aesthetic line-of-progress, as cultural expression, and by social function. These methodologies have developed successively and cumulatively: cultural expression building on aesthetic line-of-progress, social function representing a step beyond cultural expression, not its antithesis. With social function, which considers arts and artifacts not only as aesthetic objects or reflections of the spirit of their times, but also as instruments furthering the ideological foundations of society, art history has finally become the effective and prime instrument for historical research that it should always have been, revealing and analyzing those fundamental attitudes and presuppositions by which any age lives, and on which all the institutions of every society must ultimately rest.

—Alan Gowans,
*Learning to See: Historical Perspectives on
Modern Popular/Commercial Arts*

2

Material Culture and History

How history should be studied is the subject of constant discussion. At one time it tended to be confined to being a record of the doings of kings and parliaments and great figures. In more recent times, we have broadened our understanding of history to include ordinary people and everyday life. We have also, started looking at history from a comparative point of view, relating politics to social and cultural phenomena and even using quantitative methods (sizes of populations, etc.) in our analyses.

We shall understand history as being a means of interpreting what went on in the past and understanding change over time. History is an act of interpretation. We have all kinds of records about what happened in the past. Why things happened, what their significance was, and how to best understand what happened is another matter. That is why there are numerous schools of historians, who interpret various events from different perspectives (Marxist, Catholic, psychoanalytic, liberal, conservative, conflict, consensus, social, economic, etc.). Historians are, as might be expected, affected by the dominant ideas of the period in which they write. So the way historians write also tells us something.

In his classic study of medieval (fourteenth and fifteenth century) art and culture, Johan Huizinga points out how important religious thought was to the understanding of objects:

> The Middle Ages never forgot that all things would be absurd, if their meaning were exhausted in their function and their place in the phenomenal world, if by their essence they did not reach into a world beyond this. This idea of a deeper significance in ordinary things is familiar to us as well, independently of religious convictions. (Huizinga 1924,201)

The notion that things "mean" something, are what semioticians call "signs," is particularly important in the Middle Ages, which were dominated by a religious sensibility.

Huizinga, continuing this line of thinking a few paragraphs later (Huizinga, 1924, 202), quotes from William James' *Varieties of Religious Experiences*, "When we see all things in God, and refer all things to HIM, we read in common matters superior expressions of meaning." Huizinga adds:

> Here, then, is the psychological foundation from which symbolism arises. In God nothing is empty of sense: *nihil vacuum neque sine signo apud Deum*, said Saint Irenaeus. So the conviction of a transcendental meaning in all things seeks to formulate itself. About the figure of the Divinity a majestic system of correlated figures crystallizes, which all have reference to Him, because all things derive their meaning from Him. The world unfolds itself like a vast whole of symbols, like a cathedral of ideas. (Huizinga 1924,202)

In a society permeated by the religious sensibility, objects and artifacts quite naturally had a religious significance.

Not only does Huizinga stress the symbolic significance of objects, he also believes that "the true character of the spirit of an age is better revealed in its mode of regarding and expressing trivial and commonplace things than in the high manifestations of philosophy and science" (Huizinga 1924,225).

Bells, for example, had individual names and were rung in particular ways. When great events transpired, such as the election of a pope, bells rang night and day. And clothes reflected an heroic sensibility:

> The modern male costume since the end of the eighteenth century is essentially a workman's dress. Since political progress and social perfection have stood foremost in general appreciation, and the ideal itself is sought in the highest production and most equitable distribution of goods, there is no longer any need for playing the hero or the sage. . . . In aristocratic periods, on the other

hand, to be representative of true culture means to produce by conduct, by customs, by manners, by costume, by deportment, the illusion of a heroic being. (Huizinga 1924,39)

Medieval costumes (of aristocratic people) were expensive and flambuoyant—brilliantly colored and highly ornate, considerably different from the contemporary three-piece suit so common in the Western world.

Fifty years after Huizinga wrote about the importance of the commonplace, the great French historian Fernand Braudel wrote a three-volume study of "Civilization and Capitalism" whose first volume was titled *The Structures of Everyday Life*. It is everyday life, now, which is to be the subject of historical analysis. What does Braudel mean by everyday life? He explains how he uses the term in the preface to this volume:

> Everyday life consists of the little things one hardly notices in time and space. The more we reduce the focus of vision, the more likely we are to find ourselves in the environment of material life: the broad sweep usually corresponds to History with a capital letter, to distant trade troutes, and the networks of national or urban economies. If we reduce the length of time observed, we either have the event or the everyday happening. The event is, or is taken to be, unique; the everyday happening is repeated, and the more often it is repeated the more likely it is to become a generality or rather a structure. It pervades society at all levels and characterizes ways of being and behaving which are perpetuated through endless ages. (Braudel 1981,29)

This everyday life involves such things as "demography, food, costume, lodging, technology, money, towns—which are usually kept separate from one another and which develop in the margin of traditional history" (Braudel 1981,27). We are far removed, here, from a conception of history as the study of "great men" and past politics, per se.

The second chapter of Braudel's book is devoted to "Daily Bread," and is almost eighty pages long. The chapter covers such things as the cultivation of wheat and other food grains and the role they played in history. For most people, Braudel points out, bread was the basic element of their diet. Society was divided into two groups, he adds, "the few who ate meat and the many who fed on bread, gruel, roots and cooked tubers" (Braudel 1981, 106). This was because bread was much cheaper than other foods:

> In about 1780 it cost eleven times less than meat, sixty-five times less than
> fresh sea fish, nine times less than fresh-water fish, six times less than eggs,
> three times less than butter and oil. (Braudel 1981,133)

By studying the role bread played in people's lives and the development of cuisines in which other foods were utilized, Braudel was
able to obtain important insights into the lives of people and the
evolution of agriculture and the economy in France . . . and elsewhere.

There has been a change in bread eating habits in America. A
recent *Time* article entitled "Bread Goes Upper Crust" (7 May
1990, 109) points out that today consumption of of standard white
bread in America has dropped from 80 percent of total consumption to around 55 percent. Replacing this "balloon bread" are numerous variety blends "rife with cracked wheat, whole grain and
oat bran," as well as breads baked in supermarkets and other spe-
cialty bakeries.

Our interest in good bread, it is suggested, is connected to a
renewed interest in gourmet cuisine. The *Time* article quotes Eli
Zabar, owner of a New York city gourmet shop E.A.T.:

> About 15 years ago, a food revolution began in this country starting with the
> main course. Then it moved to the appetizer, then dessert. We have finally
> gotten around to bread. It's happening everywhere. (*Time*, 7 May 1990,109)

Some American bakeries have even purchased stone-lined ovens
from abroad and others have hired German bakers to come and
make bread.

Thus, the old "balloon" bread, which was so soft it could be
compressed into a small lump and then spring back into shape, is
being replaced by substantial breads, many of them fresh baked,
hard crusted, and not packaged. (The author once wrote a satirical
essay on white bread, published in *Rolling Stone*, in which he
argued that American white bread reflected our nonideological
politics whereas countries with bread with hard crusts, which
could not be scrunched up, were generally much more ideological.
This would suggest that bread has an ideological and political
significance in addition to its other meanings.)

Finally, there is a new electronic kitchen tool, the automatic
bread baker, which is becoming increasingly popular in America.

All one has to do is put the requisite ingredients into the baker and it mixes, kneads, and bakes the bread. The recipe books that come with these devices contain recipes for all kinds of gourmet and health breads as well as coffee cakes and other pastries. These devices currently cost around $300 but with economies of scale the price will probably drop considerably and automatic bread bakers will start showing up in American kitchens, alongside the now-ubiquitous microwave ovens.

The eminent historian Asa Briggs has written a book, *Victorian Things*, that deals with a number of common objects and artifacts from the Victorian period in terms of how they shed light on the dominant interests and beliefs of Victorians, eminent and ordinary. The first chapter, "Things as Emissaries," deals with the theory behind the book and with methodological questions involved in dealing with material culture.

Briggs' focus is on how people in the Victorian period regarded the objects they used: "I am more interested in nineteenth-century things as they were used and appreciated within their own context than in the things or parts of things which have survived into the twentieth century and in how we now regard them" (Briggs 1988, 14). Briggs is using material culture to understand the Victorian age as it saw itself.

An excellent example of Briggs' method is shown in his discussion of the development of the safety match, a twenty page microhistory, which is found in his chapter on "The Wonders of Common Things." In this essay, Briggs starts with the discovery of phosphor in 1699 and various devices that were used to create fire in the late 1700s and early 1800s. Safety matches were discovered by John Walker, a chemist and druggist of Stockton, England. He considered his discovery so trivial that he didn't bother to patent it. He started selling what he called "friction lights" in 1827.

He kept very detailed records and Briggs notes that Walker sold 1,836 tins of "friction lights" in 1827 and more than 12,000 by 1830. Phosphorus is a dangerous substance and Briggs mentions the deadly diseased caused by it, *phosoporus necrosis*. Eventually a new formulation was discovered and the first safety matches, made of potassium chlorate on the match heads and amorphous phosphorus on rubbing surface of the match box, were produced by a Swede, Carl Lunstrom.

By the end of the century there were twenty-five match factories in Great Britain, employing more than 4,000 workers—most of them female. In Sweden, on the other hand, a machine had been developed that could turn out 570,000 matches an hour and in America a similar machine was developed by the Diamond-Match Company. This company eventually set up some machines in England and ended up acquiring more than fifty percent interest in what had been the dominant match company in Britain, Bryant and May.

Matches made the headlines twice in the last decades of the 19th century. In 1871 Robert Lowe, Chancellor of the Exchequer, tried to impose a stamp tax on matches, without success. There was a huge outcry about the injustice of taxing the poorer elements of society, who would suffer cruelly from such a tax. There was also a match girls strike against Bryant and May in 1888 when there were economic difficulties in the match industry, a strike which Briggs suggests set a precedent for the dockers' strike of 1889.

What Briggs' history of the match shows is that even seemingly trivial and commonplace objects such as matches can be shown to play an important role in the development of societies. What is crucial is that we learn to recognize the role such objects play and the way they become woven into the fabric of social, economic, and political developments that occur in a country and, by extension, the whole world.

The focus, here, has been on particulars. Briggs explains his methodology as follows:

> My object in *Victorian Things* is to try to reconstruct "the intelligible universe"—or, more properly, universes, for there was more than one—of the Victorians; and I have never ignored the fact, though it is easy for collectors to do so, that the economic inability to transact was even more significant in Victorian Britain than the refusal to do so. In 1900/1901 only 17 per cent of the population left enough property for it to be recorded in the probate records. I have concentrated, however, as French semiologists have done, on the things that were transacted as witnesses, in my case dealing with them not through abstraction or through generalization about categories of objects and their typology—for example, clothes or milk or wine or toys—but rather through the detailed study of particular things. (Briggs 1988,31)

Briggs seems to be referring here (obliquely, in the last part of this quotation) to Roland Barthes, who has written on categories of things such as clothes, milk, wine, and toys. But Briggs also says he is emulating the work of the French semiologists, so the statement is somewhat confusing.

Whatever the case, and discussions of theory and methodology might go on endlessly, Briggs has written a masterful study of Victorian material culture which deals, from an historical perspective, with everything from matches to pens, needles to eyeglasses, stamps to cameras.

Alan Gowans has written a book, *Learning to See*, that deals with the arts from an historical perspective. In the preface to this book he discusses the fact that art history has been neglected by historians interested in studying the past:

> That orthodox political history, working by custom with written documents, would tend to use the arts and artifacts primarily or only as illustration (when at all), is perhaps understandable, if not altogether excusable. Yet intellectual history has made hardly more use of them. (Gowans 1981,3)

The reason, he suggests, is because of the methodologies that traditional art historicans have employed. These are, he adds "by an aesthetic line-of-progress, as cultural expression, and by social function" (Gowans 1981,3,4). The problem is that these methodologies have been employed only in recent years that too few historians are aware of their uses.

Gowans offers a modification of the above methodologies, based on the functions played by works of art and artifacts. The primary use of these works should be in helping to understand "certain specific and objectively recognizable functions" for society, and not basically as "vehicles for the sensibilities and expression of artists." He continues with a list describing the social functions of art: (Gowans, 17,18)

A. *Substitute Imagery*: Historic arts made substitute images of things or ideas whose memory it was desirable for some reason to preserve.

B. *Illustration*: Historic arts so related substitute images as to tell stories or record events.

C. *Beautification*: Historic arts deliberately shaped artifacts so as to make their function(s) plain to individual beholders, and thence to communities at large . . . and/or added substitute images, symbols or illustrations to artifacts so as to link them to beholders' experience and to the historical experience of communities.

D. *Persuasion/Conviction*: Historic arts deliberately "styled" artifacts so as to evoke associations with, or create metaphors of, ideologies and presuppositions (convictions) which underlie all social institutions. Historic arts thus were vehicles and instruments for transmitting those accepted values, ethics, belief systems, upon which ultimately depends the endurance of city, State and family.

What has happened, suggests Gowans, is that these functions are found in the popular arts and popular culture as well as elite forms of art and culture.

Gowans then proceeds to teach us how to see all kinds of things from this functional perspective—which is why he titled the book *Learning to See*. He is not concerned with the age-old question "is it art?" (by which we usually mean "fine" or "elite" art) but, rather, with the question of how does the work function in society and what values and ideas are reflected or contained in the work. Gowans deals with an astonishing range of topics, everything from cave drawings to Picasso's late sculptures, waxworks to Mt. Rushmore, pottery to postcards, comic strips to cars, advertisements to skyscrapers.

His reading of the significance of Barbie Dolls is particularly interesting. Dolls, he suggests, are a widespread form of substitute imagery which have a didactic function—helping children learn the conventions of their societies in terms of behavior and dress. They do this by analogical thought, since identifying these dolls as similar to themselves is within a small child's mental capacity. And "so is a mythopoetic relationship to the outside world (i.e., treating inanimate objects as if they were living, could think and talk, etc")" (Gowans 1981,75).

That is why, he explains, dolls "were invariably miniatures of adults (the baby doll only became popular c.1850, possibly in response to some aspect of the Romantic movement)" (Gowans 1981, 75). Thus, when Mattel introduced Barbie, it was returning the doll to an older and more normal social function for the doll.

There is some question about this notion in my mind. One could argue that playing with baby dolls is a means of preparing young girls for their future roles as mothers and that the switch to dolls like Barbie suggests a new definition of a woman's role, as a consumer of commodities (clothes, wigs, etc.) and as a woman who does not define herself primarily in terms of her mothering function but in terms of her relationships with others, such as Ken. (The Barbie Doll will be discussed also in the chapter on sociological analysis, so we are not done with it, by any means.) One might also study other dolls such as the Cabbage Patch Kids and play figures (since boys don't like to think of themselves as playing with dolls), such as G.I. Joe or transformers.

In adopting an historical approach to the study of artifacts it is useful to remember that we are interested in finding out what these artifacts reveal about the societies in which they are found and how the evolution and changes in these artifacts reflect, indirectly, social, economic and political changes. There are numerous questions that historians face about their discipline. How do they go beyond being purely descriptive? How do they justify their explanations? How do they justify the way they select documents, or in our case, objects, to analyze?

History is, I would suggest, an interpretative art and we have to evaluate the works of historians in terms of the quality of the arguments they make and (what seems to be) the soundness of their research. One thing is obvious. Artifacts don't change on their own account, and where we find change in the design of artifacts and objects or the development of new ones, it is because of someone thought that the change would make a better (and presumably more saleable) item. There is human agency and volition at work, and where we find that, we can make historical analyses.

One of the corollaries of the notion that culture consists of ideas is that there is no such thing as material *culture. This has caused some confusion and uneasiness among some anthropologists. People had been going out collecting pottery, projectile points, baskets, bows and arrows, and so on, and putting them in museums where curators took care of them; and they thought they were dealing with culture. Then, lo and behold, they were told that things were not culture at all. Field workers and museum curators were put in an awkward position. And the theorists were in just as bad a situation as before; for now they had to say that culture consists of ideas, the ideas cause behavior, but the behavior is not culture either; it is cultural, but not culture. And an object is the product of behavior that is cultural but not culture. So we go from culture the idea to behavior which is only cultural but not culture and then finally we arrive at a product of cultural behavior. This is, to say the least, a rather clumsy and inefficient way of dealing with the concept of culture.*

—Leslie A. White with Beth Dillingman,
The Concept of Culture

3

Anthropological Perspectives
on Material Culture

The central concept in anthropology is *culture*. In this respect, anthropology differs from history, which is generally concerned with what happened in the past and with change over time and from sociology, which focuses its attention on groups and institutions. Culture, as I shall use the term, refers to patterns of behavior and ways of thinking, beliefs, ideologies, practices, values, and so on acquired by people as members of society that are passed on from generation to generation. These beliefs and behavior patterns are often reflected in material objects and artifacts. The process by which individuals become members of a given culture is enculturation and involves communication. Some anthropologists emphasize the role ideas play in cultures while others — social anthropologists — stress the role social structures play — or, at least, insist on giving them equal importance.

For many years, anthropologists focused their attention on pre-literate groups (once called "primitive") but in recent years many anthropologists have turned their attention to modern, literate, complex societies and the various cultures and subcultures found within them. Subcultures are smaller groupings of people who exist within a larger, dominant culture, and whose beliefs, values and practices generally differ in various respects from this culture.

One topic that interests many cultural anthropologists or ethnographers (those who investigate the way other peoples see the world) is myth. From an anthropological perspective, myth refers to what might be called "sacred stories," narratives which describe the creation of the earth, the actions of deities, and related concerns. Myths are origin tales, among other things, and are tied to many practices of people in preliterate (and literate) societies. Myth in this sense must be differentiated from the common understanding of myth, which is some kind of a popularly held but erroneous notion or belief. Legends, on the other hand, will be understood as referring to the activites of mortals—great adventures of founding heroes and heroines.

Myths, Edmund Leach suggests in *Culture and Communication* are one of the ways in which metaphysical ideas are made understandable. That is, we tell stories in which "metaphysical ideas are represented by the activities of supernatural beings, magnified non-natural men and animals." The other way this is done, he adds, is to create "special material objects, buildings and spaces which serve as representations of the metaphysical ideas and their mental environment" (Leach 1976, 37).

In their quest to understand the world view of the members of a given culture or subculture, anthropologists also study their rituals—structured or what might be described as "coded" behavior patterns, often of a sacred nature, which are frequently connected to myths. These rituals, especially in preliterate societies, are often tied to important changes in the life cycle of men and women.

Ritual has the function of drawing people together, of creating a sense of solidarity or community. We might describe this function as "bonding" or unifying a group of people who may be different in various respects. That is why ritual plays such an important part in organized religion. The act of participating in a collective ritual serves to strengthen belief. Psychologically speaking, ritual tends to confirm belief; we have discovered that, paradoxically, if we act in certain ritually prescribed ways, belief generally follows. During rituals, we often make use of symbolic objects — objects which are connected to sacred myths, objects that reflect beliefs and values.

Victor Turner discusses these matters in *Dramas, Fields and Metaphors: Symbolic Action in Human Society*:

> Again, sacred objects may be shown to the novices. These may be quite simple in form like the bone, top, ball, tambourine, apples, mirror, fan, and wooly fleece displayed in the lesser Eleusinian mysteries of Athens. Such *sacra*, individually or in various combinations, may be the foci of hermeneutics or religious interpretations, sometimes in the form of myths, sometimes of gnomic utterances hardly less enigmatic than the visible symbols they purport to explain. These symbols, visual and auditory, operate culturally as mnemonics, or as communications engineers would no doubt have it, as "storage bins" of information, not about pragmatic techniques, but about cosmologies, values, and cultural axioms, whereby a society's deep knowledge is transmitted from one generation to another. (Turner 1974, 239)

The metaphor of the artifact as a "storage bin" of information is an apt one. For our job as an analyst of this artifact is to discover how it functions in its particular context and discern what it signifies or means. Rituals are particularly important in cultures without writing, where cultural traditions have to be transmitted through speech, rituals, and sacred objects.

Much of what has been discussed to this point involves an element of structuring which is why some anthropologists use the term "code" as almost synonymous with culture and focus their attention on what they call "culture codes." Earlier I quoted Edmund Leach, the distinguished social anthropologist, to the effect that the nonverbal dimensions of cultures (that is, objects and artifacts) actually can be seen as organized into patterned sets and, as such, "incorporate coded information in a manner analogous to the sounds and words and sentences of a natural language" (Leach 1976, 10). This means, he adds, we can talk about the grammatical rules that govern our use of objects (he used the example of wearing clothes) in the same way we talk about the rules that govern speech or writing.

Just as the meaning of a word is always connected to its context, so is the meaning of an object, seen as a sign (anything which can be used to stand for something else), always connected to the context or "system" of objects in which it is found. Cultures may be seen as collections of codes, codes that deal with various aspects of life and that govern behavior.

Consider cuisines which can be described as culinary codifications. Cuisines can be national, regional, and local. A cuisine is a system of rules which govern what one eats, how foods are cooked, and what dishes go with other dishes to make a satisfactory meal. In America, for example, we had (until recently, when we started worrying about our consumption of animal fats) and many people still have, a love of huge steaks. We have certain notions about how a big porterhouse steak should be cooked. The idea of *boiling a steak* causes revulsion, is somehow terribly "wrong." Why? We only boil (so the codes tell us) certain, rather tough cuts of meat, such as corned beef. Tender cuts of beef, such as porterhouse steaks, are supposed to be broiled, barbecued over charcoal or, at the very least, pan fried. Porterhouse steaks are not roasted, baked, or deep fried.

Good cuts of prime (preferably aged and marbled with fat) steak should also be served either rare or medium rare. There must be blood (the symbolic significance of which I leave to your imagination). The idea of cooking a prime cut of beef until it is well done is abhorrent to most of us—at least to middle and upper class people with a sense of style or "sophistication" about their food preferences. This would also apply to roast beef, which, conventions tell us, should be served when it is pink and bloody in the middle, if not "bleu" (blue and very rare, which is the way the French like it).

This rare charbroiled porterhouse steak is part of a classic American steak dinner—a group of specific foods, cooked in certain ways, which are deemed to go well with the steak. Thus we have our steak with either a baked potato, perhaps pan fried potatoes or with french fried potatoes, but not with mashed potatoes (okay with roast beef) or boiled potatoes.

In addition, we eat certain vegetables with steak—usually green beans. We do not, as a rule, eat vegetables such as brussel sprouts, candied carrots, or beets with a steak dinner. Our culinary codes tell us that they don't "go" with steak. Usually the steak dinner is preceded by a vegetable salad, though soup (by itself or preceding the salad) is acceptable. This salad contains lettuce, tomatoes, and other vegetables. Some restaurants feature salad bars and people might also add peppers, onions, beans, sprouts, and all kinds of other things to their salads. In America, we eat the salad before we eat the main course; in France, on the other hand, people eat their salads after the main course. We would probably drink dry red wine (not white) or beer with a steak dinner. Both would be acceptable.

All of these things I've been discussing are rule-governed; we learn various notions about food — such as what we can eat, what dishes are special treats, what we shouldn't eat — as we grow up (from our parents, from menus in restaurants, from cookbooks), develop a fondness for certain tastes when we are children, and these rules and tastes play an important role, if they don't govern, our cooking and eating for the rest of our lives. These rules about cuisines are affected, in some cases, by religious proscriptions: Baptists and Mormons won't drink liquor and Orthodox Jews won't eat meat that is not kosher. But Baptists or Mormons could substitute sparkling water for the wine and and Orthodox Jews could substitute a different cut of meat that is kosher (since a porterhouse steak is not a kosher cut) and enjoy the classic American steak dinner. Sirloin steaks are also used in classic American steak dinners but not cuts with stringy meat such as flank steak. The steak must be from a cut that is thick, tender, and juicy.

The classic American steak dinner is not just an ordinary meal. It is a celebratory one, symbolic of the wealth and abundance of American society and a means for Americans of identifying themselves with the country, its traditions and its values. This matter is especially significant when it comes to hamburgers. When an American general was released, after a number of years in Vietnam, the first thing he wanted to eat was a hamburger and a milkshake — foods that are now universally identified (thanks to the awesome success of McDonald's) with American culture and society. An English general would have requested (we may surmise) fish and chips and a French general would have asked for steak and chips.

It might even be argued that eating has ritualistic elements which explains why many religious rituals are connected to consuming food.

Ralph Linton, a distinguished anthropologist, wrote a classic article to show that many things which Americans use and which they think are "one hundred percent American" actually come from foreign countries. There is a great deal of diffusion that takes place as far as artifacts and practices are concerned that escapes our notice. In the chart that follows I list some of the artifacts Linton discusses which we think of as American and cite the actual place of origin or development of these artifacts (Berger 1974, 77,78):

ARTIFACT	PLACE OF ORIGIN OF ARTIFACT
Eiderdown quilt	Scandinavia
Glass	Egyptians
Glazed tiles	Near East
Bathtub, toilet	Romans
Soap	Gauls
Steel (in Razor)	India or Turkestan
Towel	Turkey
Fork	Italy
Spoon	Romans

His description of what we generally think of as the classic "American" breakfast is marvelous:

> If our patriot is old-fashioned enough to adhere to the so-called American breakfast, his coffee will be accompanied by an orange, domesticated in the Mediterranean region, a canteloup, domesticated in Persia, or grapes, domesticated in Asia Minor. He will follow this with a bowl of cereal made from grain domesticated in the Near East and prepared by methods also invented there. From this he will go on to waffles, a Scandinavian invention, with plenty of butter, originally a Near-Eastern cosmetic. As a side dish he will have the egg of a bird domesticated in Southeastern Asia or strips of the flesh of an animal domesticated in the same region, which have been salted and smoked by a process invented in Northern Europe. (Berger 1974, 78)

At the end of breakfast, when we read an editorial in a newspaper about the "dire results" of accepting foreign ideas, our hero "will not fail to thank a Hebrew God in an Indo-European language that he is a one hundred per cent (decimal system invented by the

Greeks) American (from Americus Vespucci, Italian geographer)"
(Berger 1974, 79).

Linton's article demonstrates the degree to which materials, artifacts, products, and practices involving these phenomena are diffused all over the world. Among our most significant contribu-
tions in recent years — as far as artifacts are concerned, that is — are
corn flakes, Coca-Cola, Levis, McDonald's hamburgers (the fast
food phenomenon), frozen foods, television sets, lasers, transis-
tors, computer chips, and microwave ovens. Americans have not
done a good job of capitalizing on their inventions, and many
consumer products, especially those of a technological nature, are
based on devices discovered in America but not exploited by them.

The diffusion of objects is heightened, also, by immigration and
by the development of tourism. As people move to other lands,
they bring with them their foods and many artifacts and objects.
Take the Italians, for example. Pizza, a regional Italian dish, is
now popular everywhere from Brazil to Israel, and so is espresso.
The popularity of this kind of coffee has led to the manufacture of
many different kinds of espresso coffee makers, from small alumi-
num "machinettas" (manufactured in Italy and used by many Italians) to expensive espresso makers from Italy, Germany, and other
countries. It has also led to the development of coffee houses that
sell beans and espresso makers, and, in some cases, espresso coffee.

In 1922, Bronislaw Malinowski published a classic book, *Argonauts of the Western Pacific*, which described and analyzed the
culture of Trobriand Islanders, inhabitants of islands off New
Guinea. The central organizing feature of Trobriand society was an
activity called the *Kula*, which Malinowski describes in the following words:

> The Kula is a form of exchange, of extensive, inter-tribal character; it is carried
> on by communities inhabiting a wide ring of islands, which form a closed
> circuit. [He then describes the route and mentions a map he has included in the
> book.] Along this route, articles of two kinds only, are constantly travelling in
> opposite directions. In the direction of the hands of a clock, moves constantly
> one of these kinds — long necklaces of red shell called *soulava*. . . . In the
> opposite direction moves the other kind — bracelets of white shell called *mwali*.
> . . . Each of these articles, as it travels in its own direction on the closed
> circuit, meets on its way articles of the other class, and is constantly being

exchanged for them. Every movement of the Kula articles, every detail of the transactions is fixed and regulated by a set of traditional rules and conventions, and some acts of the Kula are accompanied by an elaborate magical ritual and public ceremonies. (Malinowski 1922, 81)

Members of the various tribes involved in the enterprise are constantly exchanging necklaces and bracelets and, in the course of doing so, forming lifelong partnerships.

When a Trobriander gives someone a a necklace or a bracelet, he is bestowing a ceremonial gift and expects a countergift of equivalent value (this could be within minutes or up to a year). There are definite rules and codes involved in the *Kula*, one of the most central of which is that necklaces and bracelets are never moved in the wrong direction. Malinowki suggests, the institution of the *Kula* is so large and complex that none of the participants in it see it as a whole. And it is not connected to economics, since neither of the objects is of any practical use, but magic, he explains, plays an important role in the *Kula*.

It takes between two and ten years for the objects to complete a round; as they are exchanged, they bind individuals together in relationships characterized by mutual duties and obligations. Of particular interest is the fact that "customs, songs, art motives and general cultural influences travel along the *Kula* route" (Malinowski 1922, 92). The *Kula* can be seen as an institution whose function is to give meaning to the lives of the natives and Malinowki cautions us that we must be careful, in bringing modern "civilizing" beliefs to such peoples, that we don't destroy institutions and practices which make their lives meaningful.

Malinowski's study of the *Kula* can be seen as a paradigmatic analysis of the important roles that objects can play in cultures. The objects may not have much economic or utilitarian values, but they are often connected to ways of life and systems of belief that are very important to people. In analyzing objects we must remember, first, that they are often connected (indirectly and in hidden ways) to values and beliefs of great importance to people, and second, that people often don't recognize the full significance of the objects they own and use. We must learn how to assess the symbolic significance of such objects, the codes and rituals connected with them, and the way they function in the culture or subculture in which they found.

Modern people, in many respects, behave in ways similar to Malinowski's Trobriand Islanders. Consider, for example, the way Christmas is celebrated in America and many Western European (and other) countries. Gifts are ritually exchanged by people, governed by the cardinal rule in gift giving, and some would say human relationships in general, reciprocity. This matter is discussed by Sheila Johnson in an article "The Christmas Gift Horse" (Berger, 1974, 82–85).

There is a great deal of anxiety, she points out, involved in giving these gifts, with the result that Christmas is a period in which many people become distraught and even depressed. In some cases it is because of the cost of giving large numbers of people gifts, but is also is connected with the need to determine what is the proper gift (in terms of taste and expense) to give various people. If you give someone a gift that is too expensive, the recipient may be embarrassed and if the gift is too cheap, the recipient will feel slighted. The gift reflects your taste and your sense of the taste of the person given the gift. Gifts also express the nature of relationships.

Gifts, then, are "read" (as the semioticians would say) and analyzed in considerable detail in terms of what they might reflect about the giver of the gift and the receiver of the gift — and expectations that may be connected with giving and receiving gifts. Our Christmas gift giving, functionally speaking, is not terribly far removed from the exchange of necklaces and bracelets by Trobriand Islanders. Christmas gift giving, Johnson concludes, "fills a human need to reaffirm one's friendships, pay off one's obligations, and validate one's standing in the community." (Berger 1974, 85)

The Passover Seder is a feast that has been celebrated by Jews for thousands of years, marking the miraculous escape of the Jews from slavery in Egypt. The word "seder" means order, and the Passover dinner is a highly structured ritual featuring foods that have highly defined symbolic significance. A book, the Haggadah, is used which describes how the Passover feast is to be carried out and explains the meanings of the various symbolic foods and behaviors. Three plates are placed in the center of the table: one with three pieces of matzoh, one (the seder plate) with a shank bone and a roasted egg, some horse radish, celery or parsley, and some haroseth (a mixture of nuts, fruits, and wine). The third plate has a bowl of vinegar or salt water.

There is a specific order to the seder:

1. Recite the Kiddush (a prayer)
2. Wash hands
3. Eat a green vegetable
4. Break middle matzoh and hide
5. Recite Passover story
6. Wash hands before meal
7. Say certain prayers
8. Eat the bitter herb
9. Eat bitter herbs and Matzoh
10. Serve the Festival meal
11. Eat the hidden piece of Matzoh
12. Say grace
13. Recite the Hallel
14. Conclude the Seder (sing songs)

Four glasses of wine are also consumed during the ritual and play an important part in it. The Seder is a fascinating and extremely complex ritual, about which many books have been written. For our purposes, let me discuss a few of the foods and say something about their symbolic significance.

Object	SYMBOLIC Significance
Matzoh (unleavened bread)	Jews in Egypt hadn't time to let bread rise
Bitter Herbs	Bitter life Jews led in Egypt
Bitter Herbs and Matzoh	Remembrance of the Temple

One thing that should be pointed out is that during the Seder, when Jews eat bitter herbs, they identify personally with the ancient Jews who escaped from Egypt and participate, existentially, in the escape. As the Haggadah says:

> In every generation one must look upon himself as if he personally had come out from Egypt, as the Bible says "And thou shalt tell thy son on that day, saying, it is because of that which the Eternal did to me when I went forth from Egypt."

The bitter herbs, then, are very powerful symbols which remind Jews of the plight of their ancestors and help contemporary Jews identify with the Jews in Egypt. The Seder is, in actuality, a festive occasion — one in which groups of people celebrate together with a very lovely meal. And, in doing so, they "relive" the events of one of their escapes from bondage and reestablish their ties to their religion and to one another. This ritual, and others like it in Judaism, have probably played an important role in helping Jews survive and maintain a distinct identity as a people, living as a minority amongst other peoples, through the millenia.

Objects are symbolic when they are connected ritualistically and mythically (sometimes through unconscious association) to events of significance for individuals, groups of people (connected by race, religion, occupation, ethnicity, etc.) and nations. The task of the anthropological analyst of material culture is to see the role that various objects play in the most important myths and rituals of specific cultures and subcultures and the manner in which all of these relate to dominant values and beliefs.

Bobby Clark has developed almost a scientific system on the basis of the limp, soft walking stick with which he periodically threatens an attractive female on the stage. . . . The furry walking stick as a phallic symbol is a masterful, truly creative combination of fantastic disguise and obvious exhibitionism. Just because of its daring it is laugh-provoking. Here lies its great communicative truth: neither the artist who had the idea nor the onlooker who enjoys the act with intense pleasure may be conscious of the underlying meaning; it may remain unconscious in both actor and audience. For full enjoyment and understanding, it is not necessary that the symbolic meaning of the furry walking stick enter anyone's consciousness. The communication remains deeply and totally on an unconscious level.

—Martin Grotjahn,
Beyond Laughter: Humor and the Subconscious

4

Psychoanalytic Analysis of Material Culture

When we hear the term "psychoanalysis" we usually think of the subject in relation to neurotic behavior and Freud's remarkable writings. But psychoanalytic theory has been applied, with considerable success, to history, anthropology, sociology, political science, literary criticism and culture studies, and many other forms of intellectual endeavor as well. Freud has listed, in an essay titled "Psychoanalysis," what he considers to be the cornerstones of the theory (reprinted in a book of Freud's essays, *Character and Culture*, edited by Philip Rieff 1963, 244):

> The assumption that there are unconscious mental processes, the recognition of the theory of resistance and repression, the appreciation of the importance of sexuality and of the Oedipus Complex—these constitute the principal subject-matter of psychoanalysis and the foundation of its theory.

Each of these concepts is very complex, and many of them are misunderstood, but they give a broad picture of the general contours of the science.

For example, Freud's notion of sexuality is much broader than what we would understand as genital sex. He writes, in the same essay that

It became necessary to enlarge the concept of what was sexual until it covered more than the impulsion of the two sexes in the sexual act or towards provoking particular pleasurable sensations in the genitals. (Rieff 1963,240)

In his enlargement of the concept of sexuality, he dealt with infantile sexuality, normal (from his particular perspective) sexuality and what he described as "perverse" sexuality. We must recognize, in passing, that this essay of Freud's was written in 1922, when attitudes towards sexuality relative to normalcy and perversion were much different from what they are now. His analysis of the sexual instinct, what he called the libido, is of particular interest.

Freud argued that as people develop they pass through a number of sexual stages. In *An Elementary Textbook of Psychoanalysis*, Charles Brenner describes the stages:

For the first year and a half of life, approximately, the mouth, lips and tongue are the chief sexual organs of the infant. By this we mean that its desires as well as its gratifications are primarily oral ones. . . . In the next year and a half, the other end of the alimentary canal, that is the anus, comes to be the most important site of sexual tensions and gratifications. . . . Toward the close of the third year of life the leading sexual role begins to be assumed by the genitals, and it is normally maintained by them thereafter. This phase of sexual development is referred to as the phallic one for two reasons. In the first place, the penis is the principal object of interest to the child of either sex. In the second, we believe that the little girl's organ of sexual excitement and pleasure during this period is her clitoris, which is embryonically the female analogue of the penis. (Brenner 1974,24)

When children reach puberty, they learn to focus their sexuality, generally on members of the opposite sex, in a stage known as the genital stage.

The young boy's interest in his penis is connected to the development of the Oedipus Complex, a powerful love affair which is for many people, Brenner suggests, "the most intense affair of their entire lives." (1974, 106)

What Freud described as the Oedipus Complex involves an unconscious desire, in young boys between two and five generally speaking, for the mother and an accompanying hostility towards the father. (In the same light, young girls wish to supplant their mothers, but the way this matter works out is different from boys.) This feeling is quite normal, Freud points out, and most people are able to master it. Boys do this by developing an anxiety about being castrated, a phenomenon known as "castration anxiety." The Oedipus Complex, Freud believed, was of the greatest importance in determining the nature of a person's erotic life, and failure to master the Oedipus Complex was, Freud suggested, at the core of neuroses.

We might use this typology on sexual development to classify artifacts (based on their function and symbolic significance). Thus, certain artifacts would have, primarily, an oral significance, others an anal, phallic, or genital one.

Oral	Anal	Phallic	Genital
baby bottle	potty	video game joystick	
milk	chocolate bar	champagne bottle	aphrodisiac
toothbrush	enema	condom	vibrator
pipe		cigar	

Freud points out that there is a remarkable similarity in German between the word for cocoa (Kacoa) and feces (Kahkah), so the notion that chocolate bars, cocoa, etc. are "anal" should not strike one as too remarkable, even though this is a culturally based matter.

This Oedipal desire is, of course, repressed. Repression involves barring unconscious, instinctual wishes, memories and desires from consciousness without being aware of doing so. Freud said we "withdraw interest" in these phenomena. This is done automatically and is not connected to acts of will or anything like that. This process of repression is generally considered the most basic defense mechanism, the term given to all attempts by the ego to control instincts and fend off anxieties. If one tries to get at this repressed material, one meets with resistance, an unconsciously drawn and almost impenetrable wall around the repressed material. Thus, we repress knowledge of the sexual dimensions and functions of objects and of their relation to various defense mechanisms. Psychoanalysis was the term Freud gave to this interpretative science. As Freud writes,

> It was a triumph of the interpretative art of psychoanalysis when it succeeded in demonstrating that certain common mental acts of normal people, for

which no one had hitherto attempted to put forward a psychological explanation, were to be regarded in the same light at the symptoms of neurotics: that is to say, they had a *meaning*, which was unknown to the subject but which could easily be discovered by analytic means. . . . A class of material was brought to light which is calculated better than any other to stimulate a belief in the existence of unconscious mental acts in people to whom the hypothesis of something at once mental and unconscious seems strange and even absurd. (Rieff 1963, 235-6)

We are not aware of everything in our minds because we repress a great deal of material and place it in our unconscious — for a variety of reasons.

Freud's theory of the unconscious, known as his "Topographical theory," posits three areas in the mind. A useful analogy to use is an iceberg. The part of the iceberg we can see above sea level (which is a relatively small portion of the iceberg) is the conscious aspect of our minds. The area just below sea level, in which we can dimly make out the contours of the iceberg, would be what Freud called the pre-conscious areas of the mind. And the major part of the iceberg, which we cannot see, because it is buried in darkness, would correspond to what would be called our unconscious.

Material can move from preconsciousness to consciousness, but not from unconsciousness to consciousness, because of repression. The barrier between unconsciousness and consciousness cannot be breached, ordinarily. Only psychologists, studying the symbolism in our dreams and spending a great deal of time with us in therapy (what is called "the talking cure") can get at this unconscious material.

Our interest, as analysts of material culture, is not in the repressed contents of a neurotic's mind, but in the way an artifact relates to (or perhaps reflects) unconscious needs and desires we have. This can be on a personal or a cultural level. Objects are often, unconsciously, connected to various anxieties and fears we have and offer us, and in some cases promise us, all kinds of psychic rewards and gratifications. It is important that we understand the way they do these things if we are to avoid being dominated by them. There are people, we must remember, who are compulsive shoppers and cannot resist buying things — things they don't need and which they often can't afford.

At the conscious level, these shoppers purchase things because they want them. At the unconscious level, among other reasons, they buy things because of a need to demonstrate their power to choose, to have good things. They are probably suffering from what Freud called a "repitition compulsion," a need to repeat certain behaviors because of the unconscious gratifications they provide.

In his *Handbook of Consumer Motivations: The Psychology of the World of Objects*, Ernest Dichter provides a fascinating analysis of the various reasons people use cigarette lighters. We can fit his analysis into Freud's topographical hypothesis. At the conscious level, we use lighters to light cigarettes, cigars, or pipes. At the preconscious level, we use them because of a desire for mastery and power, reflected in our ability to summon fire. This is connected, he suggests, to the role fire has played throughout history and is reflected in the legend of Prometheus, who gave fire to mankind.

It is at the unconscious level that cigarette lighters are most interesting. After discussing cigarette lighters at what we would describe as the conscious and preconscious levels, Dichter writes:

> Research evidence suggests that at a still deeper level the need for certainty that a cigarette lighter will work matters as much as it does because it is also bound up with the idea of sexual potency. The working of the lighter becomes a kind of symbol of the flame which must be lit in consumating sexual union. (Dichter 1964,341)

Objects, then, may function at different levels and one of the tasks of the psychoanalytic interpreter of material culture is to discover, to the extent this is possible, the unconscious reasons we buy and use objects.

Freud later developed his "Structural Hypothesis" which suggested how the mind works. This is described by Charles Brenner in *An Elementary Textbook of Psychoanalysis* (1974, 35) as follows:

> We may say that id comprises the psychic representatives of the drives, the ego consists of those functions which have to do with the individual's relation to his environment, and the superego comprises the moral precepts of our minds as well as our ideal aspirations.
>
> The drives, of course, we assume to be present from birth, but the same is certainly not true of interest in or control of the environment on the one hand, nor of any moral sense or aspirations on the other. It is obvious that neither of

the latter, that is neither the ego nor the superego develops till sometime after birth.

Freud expressed this fact by assuming that the id composed the entire psychic apparatus at birth, and that they ego and superego were originally parts of the id which differentiated sufficiently in the course of growth to warrant their being considered as separate functional entities.

The ego is constantly trying to balance the desires of the id and the demands of the superego. If the ego is strong enough to maintain harmony, a person can function tolerably well in society. But people who are id dominated are so much the prisoners of their impulses and desires that they cannot defer gratifications long enough to get good educations and cause all kinds of problems for society and themselves. Superego dominated people, on the other hand, are so overwhelmed by guilt that they have severe problems. One needs a certain amount of id to have energy and a certain amount of superego to be able to restrain one's impulses; too much of either creates problems.

Freud's "Structural hypothesis" may also be used to set up a typology to interpret and understand material culture. Certain artifacts, the argument goes, would have a primarily id function while others would primarily have ego or superego functions.

Id	Ego	Superego
Playboy magazine	Textbooks	the Bible
Bikini	Scientist's White Coat	Clerical garb
Barbie Doll	Science Set	Book of Fables
Champagne Flute	Microscope	Holy Water Vessel

One might extend this chart considerably. What it does is show the extent to which objects often are connected to aspects of our psyches — connections which we may not have thought of previously (or which we may have recognized and repressed).

One way the ego tries to maintain equilibrium is through the use of various defense mechanisms. I have already discussed repression. Let me briefly describe some of the other common defense mechanisms, because we may find them useful when making psychoanalytic interpretations of material culture. These definitions will draw on the discussions in Brenner's book, *An Elementary Textbook of Psychoanalysis*:

Suppression. This is a conscious decision to put something out of our minds. Since this was consciously done, it can be recalled with relative ease (unlike repression, which was an unconscious act). This is generally thought to be the second most basic defense mechanism, after repression.

Reaction Formation. One of a pair of ambivalent feelings (example: hate) is made unconscious and kept that way by overemphasizing the other feeling (in this case, love). In trying to understand reaction formation, we always have to determine what the ego fears and what it is trying to accomplish. One problem with this concept is that it allows us to interpret anything two ways. If we see something we would ordinarily described as "love" or "hate" or "jealousy," are we seeing reaction formations against their opposites or the genuine behavior? The answer is that we have to look at the situation, the role of the ego and related matters.

Undoing. This describes an action or thought which "undoes" something done or thought previously. Much ritualistic behavior in children and adults is connected consciously (and unconsciously) with undoing—attempts by the ego to "undo" id-dominated thoughts and behavior.

Denial. This is an unwillingness to accept the reality of some thought or action that generates anxiety by means of a wish-fulfilling fantasy or by behavior. Denial is connected to play and daydreaming and is the basis of our sense that recreational activities are good ways of escaping from the burdens of everyday existence.

Projection. Here an individual attributes to some other individual some wish or impulse that is his own. We attempt to deny some hostile or aggressive feeling we have towards someone by attributing these feelings to that person. This occurs in normal people and is not only seen in neurotics and psychotics, though projection generally is seen in our early years.

Identification. This refers to our desire to become like someone we admire in some aspect of thought or of behavior. We see this, for example, with young children "imitating" adults and with adolescents who dress and talk like movie stars or athletic heroes.

Fixation. In this process, one becomes obsessively preoccupied or attached to some person or mode of gratification (such as an oral or an anal one). Often it is connected to traumatic experiences. It is a perfectly normal form of behavior, though it can be of such magnitude that it is dysfunctional and connected to mental illness.

Regression. This refers to returning to some earlier mode or object of gratification, often as a means of dealing with some anxiety provoking situation. In times of stress, adults may derive pleasure from eating ice cream cones (an oral form of gratification).

Rationalization. Here a person offers "reasonable" excuses or explanations for behavior that is really motivated by unconscious forces.

Ambivalence. This is a simultaneous feeling of both love and hate or attraction and repulsion toward some person or object. In some cases, the feelings alternate in great rapidity, allowing people the opportunity to gratify contradictory wishes or feelings.

Sublimation. This denotes a substitute form of action that is socially acceptable and gives a degree of unconscious gratification to infantile drive derivatives which have been rejected in their original form. Artistic activity is often held to be a sublimation of sexual drives. Sublimation is not really a defense mechanism, per se, but it functions in an analagous manner and if often included in lists of defense mechanisms.

Let me offer a couple of examples of how we can use the defense mechanisms to interpret material culture. I have already mentioned that we often derive pleasure by eating foods connected with our earlier days, when demands on us were not as great. If we look at the development of video games, we find that the first action games were of the "Space Invader" genre. The game involved guiding rocket ships around through outer space and firing guns at invading aliens, an activity that can be described as phallic.

In Pac-Man, which was the most popular video game for a number of years, the game was based on devouring dots, a kind of behavior that is oral and which thus represents a regression, caused, I would suggest, by unconscious feelings of anxiety Americans (of all ages) felt about their place in the world.

The huge collection of shoes that Imelda Marcos had, something like 2000 pairs, suggests some kind of a fixation on these objects. She, of course, rationalized her behavior arguing she was trying to help the Phillipino shoe industry. Posters of movie stars or sports heroes and heroines might be good examples of identification; young people put these posters up in their rooms and identify with them. A teenage daughter of a friend of mine plastered her room with posters and pictures of Marilyn Monroe and objects (dolls, statuettes) related to her and her films.

It is perfectly normal for people to use these defense mechanisms in coping with anxiety and the tribulations of day-to-day living; they are not reflections of neuroses except when used to excess and distorted from their traditional functions.

It is Freud's writing about sexual symbols that lead some people to describe his theories (in general) as far-fetched and ridiculous. Psychoanalytically inclined thinkers would suggest that a number of these people do not really understand Freud's highly complex theories and quite likely have not read very much Freud. And there may be an element of repression involved. Of course there are many people who are quite familiar with Freud's theories and still find them untenable, for a variety of reasons. They might, for example, consider his theory to be unverifiable or one that can't be proven wrong. Whatever the case, Freud's analysis of symbols which is connected to his theory of dreams, is fascinating and has great utility, I believe, in making sense of material culture.

In his masterpiece, *The Interpretation of Dreams*, published in 1901, Freud discusses the indirect way we represent things. (In dreams we disguise sexual symbols so the dreams will not alert the dream censor, superego, which will wake up the dreamer.) This symbolization as Freud points out:

> is not peculiar to dreams, but is characteristic of unconscious ideation, in particular among people, and it is to be found in folklore, and in popular

myths, legends, linguistic functions, proverbial wisdom and current jokes, to a more complete extent than in dreams. (Freud 1965,386)

After discussing a number of reservations and qualifications concerning his theory of symbolization, Freud goes on to discuss some of the more common representations, in dreams, of male and female sexual organs. Freud pointed out, I might add, that every analysis of the meaning of symbols found in a dream has to focus on a specific dream of an individual. You cannot assume that a symbol (except in the broadest sense) always means the same thing in all dreams.

Here is what Freud writes about dream symbolization:

> All elongated objects, such as sticks, tree-trunks and umbrellas . . . stand for the male organ . . . as well as all long, sharp weapons such as knives, daggers and pikes . . . Boxes, cases, chests, cupboards and ovens represent the uterus . . . and also hollow objects, ships, and vessels of all kinds. . . . Rooms in dreams are usually women . . . if the various ways in and out of them are represented, this interpretation is scarcely open to doubt. (Freud 1965,389)

In *A General Introduction to Psychoanalysis* (1953, 162) Freud adds to the list of phallic symbols items those which have the property of penetrating such as *"knives, daggers, lances, sabres . . . guns, pistols and revolvers.* Others he includes are *"taps, water cans, or springs . . .* [and] other objects which are capable of elongation such as *pulley lamps, pencils.*

The female genitalia, in turn, are represented by (1953, 162) objects with "the property of enclosing a space or . . . of acting as receptacles: such as *pits, hollows and caves*, and also *jars and bottles . . . wood, paper*, and objects made of these such as *tables and books.*" In addition, Freud lists churches, chapels, apples, peaches, and fruit in general, woods and thickets, and so on.

Sexual intercourse is represented in dreams by activities such as dancing, riding, climbing, experiencing some act of violence, sliding, gliding, falling. In all cases, we find disguises, so that unconscious wishes can be fullfilled in dreams without interruption or cessation.

What Freud has done is to find phenomena which represent or are analagous to male and female genitals in terms of function or design (penetrative or receptive). These phallic symbols and symbols of the uterus are often, semiotically speaking, iconic — that is, they resemble, visually speaking, the organs they represent. Freud offers long and highly complicated discussions of his theory of symbolization and the function of symbols in dreams. Readers interested in this subject are encouraged to read relevant sections of *The Interpretation of Dreams* or *A General Introduction of Psychoanalysis*.

I would like to suggest that Freud's ideas about sexual symbols need not be confined to dreams or folklore or other forms of artistic expression, but can be applied to many artifacts and objects in the real world. For example, kitchen appliances might be seen to have "sexual identities" — some are incorporative (refrigerators, microwave ovens, dishwashers) and others are penetrating (mixers, electric knives).

In *Paradoxes of Everyday Life*, psychiatrist Milton R. Saperstein offers a discussion of clocks that is relevant. He analyzes clocks, which he suggests can be seen as symbols of female genitals:

> Its hidden machinery is easily equated with those recessed and thus mysterious organs and its rhythmical movement is reminiscent of their periodic activity. There are women so obsessed by their genitalia that they put clocks all over the house or, conversely, hesitate to display even one. These different ways of handling the same obsession depend on the varying patterns of exhibitionism in the women concerned. (Sapirstein 1955,98)

Sapirstein offers another example of a woman who was so preoccupied with her bowel movements that when she decorated her house, without being aware of what she was doing, she turned her whole house into "a gigantic bathroom." She painted all the walls white, used curtains of a transparent plastic material, and placed white, decorative bowls all over. She even put a small fountain in what had been a fireplace.

None of this behavior or the behavior of women Sapirstein

writes about is conscious or recognized on the part of the women involved. It is because of the unconscious significance of artifacts and objects (such as furniture, drapes, clocks, etc.) and because in America the wife's family often assists in the decorating of homes, that decorating a home, Sapirstein tells us, is one of the times when a woman is most apt "to go to pieces."

Freud wrote dozens of books explacating his ideas and the literature on psychoanalytic thought is immense. There are many other theorists whose work bears investigating — Jung, Adler, Fromm, Horney, Bettelheim, Kris; one could go on endlessly. Some of these theorists disagree with Freud on various points, some basically agree but make modifications here and there.

My goal in this chapter is to suggest that there are often unconscious attitudes, motivations, and beliefs which affect the way we relate to material culture. I need only cite the matter of the way people purchase cars to make my point. (Dichter discusses the irrational aspects of car purchases in considerable detail in *The Engineering of Consent*.) If I have alerted readers to the possibility that our decisions about what we buy and use are based, often and to a great degree, on unconscious matters, my purpose will have been served. I have also provided a number of psychoanalytic concepts that can be used in interpreting artifacts from a psychoanalytic perspective, should the reader be inclined to do so.

Now, when a commodity is sold, the consumer not only pays for its styling and the name made famous through advertising, but also for the styling of the selling process. As far as the commodity is concerned, conscious efforts are made to shift the emphasis from the specific commodity to the experience of consumption.

Ultimately the aesthetization of commodities means that they tend to dissolve into enjoyable experiences, detached from the commodity itself. The tendency to sell these processes as material/immaterial types of commodities leaves no time to consider their use-value. By selling the commodity in the form of absolute consumption, the market remains unsatiated.

To establish this trend, it is not enough to mould and remould the army of sellers; one must condition the instincts and behavior of the "public at large." And since young people are easiest to to manipulate, they become the instrument and expression of a general trend towards moulding.

— W. F. Haug, Critique of Commodity Aesthetics:
Appearance, Sexuality and Advertising in Capitalist Society

5

Marxist Analysis of Material Culture

One of the central concepts in Marxism is that the economic relations that obtain in a society shape, but do not determine, the
dominant institutions found in that society. And these institutions,
such as the church, the education system, the arts, the legal system, shape the consciousness of individuals who live in that society. As Marx wrote in his *Preface to a Contribution to the Critique
of Political Economy*:

> In the social production which men carry on they enter into definite relations
> that are indispensable and independent of their will; these relations of produc-
> tion correspond to a definite state of development of their material powers of
> production. The totality of these relations of production constitutes the eco-
> nomic structure of society—the real foundation, on which legal and political
> superstructures arise and to which definite forms of social consciousness cor-
> respond. The mode of production of material life determines the general
> character of the social, political and spiritual processes of life. It is not con-
> sciousness of men that determines their being, but, on the contrary, their social
> being determines their consciousness. (Marx 1964,51)

This mode of production is the "base" and the social institutions
that are shaped by it form the "superstructure."

There are some Marxist thinkers, "vulgar Marxists," who believe
that the base determines, in very precise ways, the superstructure,

but this kind of thinking is not very common among Marxists today. It would mean that all societies that are at similar stages of economic development would have the same cultural institutions, a position that is not tenable. Vulgar Marxism is sometimes equated with Stalinist thinking, which many Marxists consider to be a perversion of Marx's ideas.

It is the creation of the material culture that, so the argument goes, shapes the economic order and, ultimately, the consciousness of individuals. In order to manufacture clothes, furniture, automobiles, appliances, machines of one sort or another, we need factories and a huge industrial base. Ironically, then, it is the economic system hidden behind the artifacts and objects we purchase that plays so important a role in shaping our consciousness of ourselves and the world. People, of course, play an important role in the creation of ideas and beliefs, but, so the argument goes, they are affected by the economic and social conditions found in the societies in which they live.

Materialist philosophy is a response to idealist philosophy, which stresses the importance of ideas. Hegel, the great German philosopher, had developed a system of thought which was dialectical, but idealist. He stressed the importance of ideas. His system of thought worked as follows (in rough outline). An idea or what might be called a *thesis* led (via the dialectical process) to an opposing idea, an *antithesis* that led, in turn to a combination of the two opposing ideas, a *synthesis*. This synthesis, in turn, became a thesis and engendered yet another antithesis and the process continued on at great length, until it finally ended in the development of the nation state. Marx turned Hegel "upside down" as some have put it, and substituted the working classes or proletariat for the thesis, the owners of the means of production or bourgeoisie for the antithesis and the development of communism as the synthesis, which ended the dialectical process. This is because history is class conflict and when you get rid of classes you "end" history, so to speak.

There are two classes, then, which are locked in combat, until a communist society is formed (usually after a revolution in which the proletariat overthrows the bourgeoisie and seizes the economic institutions in the name of the people). As Marx wrote:

The history of all hitherto existing society is the history of class struggle. Freeman and slave, patrician and plebeian, lord and serf, guild-master and journeyman, in a world oppressor and oppressed, stood in constant opposition to one another, carried on an uninterrupted, now hidden, now open, fight, a fight that each time ended either in a revolutionary reconstitution of society at large, or in the common ruin of the contending classes. (Marx 1964,200)

It is in the interest of the bourgeoisie to prevent the proletariat from developing class consciousness and an awareness of itself as an exploited class and one that has the power, through force of numbers, to seize control of society and reshape economic and social institutions so they will serve the needs of the masses.

The bourgeoisie maintains its control by diverting the proletariat via a modern equivalent of the Roman "bread and circuses" ploy. The bourgeoisie provides enough bread (read "food" and some of the good things of life) so large numbers of people aren't in desperate circumstances and enough games (read entertainments, mass media, etc.) so the proletariat is diverted and doesn't spend much time thinking about the way it is being exploited.

The bourgeoisie, in owning the means of production of goods, also controls the production of ideas, which is why, he argues, the ideas of the ruling classes inevitably are the ideas of the masses:

The ideas of the ruling classes are, in every age, the ruling ideas: i.e. the class which is the dominant *material* force in society is at the same time its dominant *intellectual* force. The class which has the means of material production at its disposal, has control at the same time over the means of mental production, so that in consequence the ideas of those who lack the means of mental production are in general, subject to it. The dominant ideas are nothing more than the ideal expression of the dominant material relationships, the dominant material relationships grasped as ideas, and thus of the relationships which make one class the ruling one; they are consequently the ideas of its dominance. (Marx 1964,78)

Among the ideas which the ruling class seeks to inculcate in the masses is the notion that one's fate is entirely in one's own hands, or, to put it another way, success is a function of willpower and not accidents of birth into one class or another. This notion, and others like it which justify the status quo, is part of what Marxists describe as "false consciousness," mistaken ideas which the proletariat has about itself and its possibilities. These follow in the paragraphs below:

Everyone, in principle, has an equal chance to succeed — as the numerous stories of people who were born poor and became multimillionaires demonstrates. Besides, over time, wealthy families will disintegrate since, as everyone knows, it's "shirtsleeves to shirtsleeves in three generations." In addition, the ruling class argues that inequality is natural, not historical. All societies, and even animal groupings, exhibit hierarchy in one form or another — whether it be the aristocracy, celebrities, or "big chiefs." Even hens have a pecking order. Egalitarian philosophies, such as Marxism, so the argument goes, run counter to nature and are doomed.

In America, for a long time, large numbers of people thought (so surveys indicated) we had achieved a "classless, all-middle class" society, with just a few people at the top of the economic pyramid and a relatively small percentage of poor people, living in "pockets of poverty" (most of whom would be moved into the middle classes without too much difficulty) at the bottom. It is, obviously, in the interest of members of the ruling class to play down class differences, a process called mystification, and to foster illusions, among the proletariat, about its status and possibilities.

These beliefs, which further the interests of the ruling classes, form what Marx described as an "ideology," and that, roughly speaking, is a logically coherent and widely applicable set of sociopolitical beliefs. The ruling class actually believes these ideas; they do not develop this ideology cynically. At one time most Marxists argued that the ruling classes used ideological beliefs to manipulate people and really "knew better" but most Marxists no longer accept the manipulation thesis. Why should the bourgeoisie not believe in its ideology, when its ideas dominate and justify maintaining the status quo. People's ideas and behaviors are manipulated, but the manipulation (or shaping) is not done consciously, that is.

The German Marxist Wolfgang Fritz Haug provides numerous examples of the power of the bourgeoisie to shape people's consciousness in his book *Critique of Commodity Aesthetics: Appearance, Sexuality and Advertising in Capitalist Society*, published in German in 1971 and in English in 1986. Haug argues that capitalism exploits and often manipulates human sensuality in selling products. He defines his understanding of aesthetics as follows: (Haug 1986, 8)

The term "commodity aesthetics," specifically, narrows it [aesthetics] down in two respects: on the one hand to "beauty," i.e. an appearance which appeals to the senses; and, on the other hand, to a beauty developed in the service of the realization of exchange-value, whereby commodities are designed to stimulate in the onlooker the desire to possess and the impulse to buy. In so far as that which is beautiful about a commodity appeals to people, it engages their sensual understanding and the sensual interest which in turn determines it. The transformation of the world of useful objects into commodities triggers instinctual responses, and the functional means by which not only the world of sensual objects but also human sensuality itself is remolded again and again.

As an example, he discusses how a German advertising campaign for underwear pushed men into having a "new standard in men's relationship with their bodies" (Haug 1986, 82). The campaign set out to convince German men to change their underwear daily and used images of German men with heads of pigs (those who didn't change their underwear daily) to make its point, exploiting their insecurity and feelings of guilt about their bodies. In a similar vein, a German cosmetics company exploited narcissism among adolescents and young men and anxieties of older men about being old (or perhaps not youthfully masculine would be more accurate) in its advertising campaign.

In *The Mechanical Bride*, Marshall McLuhan has an analysis of the symbolic significance of Charlie McCarthy, Edgar Bergen's famous dummy, that is interesting. McCarthy is always cocky and rebellious, telling Bergen that he's going to sever relations with Bergen and run off with some guest movie star who is on the program. But what all this really reflects, McLuhan argues, is the illusion of freedom (on Charlie McCarthy's part) and the existence of real authority:

There is no mistaking those muted and forbearing tones of Bergen for anything but power. His quiet, neutral patience with the raucous and querulous McCarthy embodies the relationship between the average man and the impersonal agencies of social control in a technological world. And the situation of Charlie the dummy is a very accurate reflection of the paradox of the individual of Big Town. The more he becomes drunk with the power that flows through and around him, the more he is recalled to his helpless dummy status. The louder his rebellious ravings, the more the mouthpiece he. (McLuhan 1967,16)

Charlie's numerous digs, his insults, his nasty comments about Bergen, are only means of allowing him to vent his rage harmlessly (that is, not against the class system in the case of people) and function to give him psychological gratifications and the illusion of power. McCarthy, then, is a paradigmatic figure – a symbol of the common man and woman, who are misguided by illusions they have about themselves and do not recognize the extent to which they are controlled and manipulated (in Charlie's case, literally). The puppet metaphor may be too strong but it does reflect, Marxist culture theorists would argue, the way people are misguided about themselves and their possibilities and the extent to which people's consciousness (and behavior) are affected by the economic conditions that obtain in society.

Adrian Forty also talks about the role of illusion in his book, *Objects of Desire: Design and Society from Wedgwood to IBM.* Forty's book is a study of material culture and of the role capitalism has played in shaping the design of household objects, furniture, machines, and many other things. He uses the term "commodity fetishism" to explain why people desire to possess objects:

> The belief that unusual or unique possessions bestow individuality upon their owners is an illusion that has been indulged in for a long time. This aspect of commodity fetishism was presumably derived from the aristocratic practice of collecting relics, curiosities and unique works of art, but how manufactured goods, by their nature never unique, ever came to be regarded in the same light is mysterious. Whatever the case, capitalist manufacture was quick to take advantage of it, and produce ten, twenty or a hundred designs where one would have sufficed. (Forty 1986,87)

These designs, and all changes in the design of manufactured objects, Forty adds, are done, ultimately, to make bigger profits for manufacturers (or those who use the products) and are not the result of the free expression of imagination and creativity on the part of some designer.

As an example Forty discusses computers. Their sleek, modern designs are meant to foster illusions in office workers about their status and the kind of work they are doing. Many modern offices have carpeted floors, good-looking furniture and tasteful colors, all of which suggest, to the workers, that their work is "clean" and that work in such offices, surrounded by good-looking objects, is, somehow, pleasurable. We now have computers which monitor the number of keystrokes of word processors which leads to incredible stress, and a high turnover rate in this field. The illusion of "clean" work at a trendy office masks the reality of surveillance, second-by-second supervision, and of a number of physical ailments that stem from typing continuously and exposure to monitor screens.

Alienation is probably the central concept in classical Marxist thought and many Marxists see alienation as the basic problem in capitalist societies. Marx describes alienation as follows:

> In what does this alienation of labour consist? First, that the work is *external* to the worker, that is not part of his nature, that consequently he does not fulfill himself in his work but denies himself, has a feeling of misery, not of wellbeing, does not develop freely a physical and mental energy, but is physically exhausted and mentally debased. His work is not voluntary but imposed, *forced labour*. It is not the satisfaction of a need, but only a *means* for satisfying other needs. Its alien character is shown by the fact that as soon as there is no physical or other compulsion it is avoided like the plague. Finally, the alienated character of work for the worker appears in the fact that it is not his work but work for someone else, that in work he does not belong to himself but to another person. . . .
>
> The *alienation* of the worker in his product means not only that labour becomes an object, takes on its own existence, but that it exists outside him, independently, and alien to him, and that it stands opposed to him as an autonomous power. (Marx 1964,169–70)

People become, Marx argues, estranged from themselves and workers experience themselves as "objects" which are acted upon and not subjects who initiate actions and are active forces in society. What workers produce are commodities, objects separated from their productive labor and workers ultimately feel that they, too, are commodities . . . self-acting and self-conscious ones.

In such circumstances, people seek momentary gratifications and relief. They find gratifications and diversion from the mass media and they find relief from feelings of self-estrangement and powerlessness by purchasing things. Alienation is functional for capitalists in that it generates (aided by advertising) impulsive and endless consumption. Marx wrote about how people in capitalist societies worked to create new needs in people—a better term might be desires—in order to get them (Marx used the term "force") to purchase new products and services. Needs are finite; desires are infinite. And it is advertising, more than anything else, which stimulates desire in people and manipulates this desire to sell things.

The French Marxist Henri LeFebvre argues, in *Everyday Life in the Modern World*, that we now live in a "Bureaucratic Society of Controlled Consumption," a stage in capitalist development that he suggests is characterized by a diffused and hard to pin down kind of "terror" (generated by class differences and the force required to maintain such differences) and in which advertising plays an important role. As he writes:

> In France, there is *nothing* — whether object, individual or social group — that is *valued* apart from its double, the image that advertises and sanctifies it. This image *duplicates* not only an object's material, perceptible existence but desire and pleasure that it makes into fictions situating them in the land of make-believe, promising "happiness" — the happiness of being a consumer. (LeFebvre 1984,105)

Advertising does this by mythologizing products, showing how they help enhance a person's life (by creating and then doing away with anxieties we have about ourselves) and, in particular, relationships with others. It is these mythologies which Barthes analyzes (for France) in *Mythologies* and which Marshall McLuhan analyzes (for America) in *The Mechanical Bride*.

Advertising has a number of other functions. For one thing, it focuses our attention on our own lives (it is narcissistic) and distracts our attention from social and political considerations. It has, then, a privatizing function. It also tends to support the class system and social relations that obtain in a given society, and thus has a legitimating function. The fact that people have access to so many goods, except for those living in poverty, implies that the social-economic system is good and should be maintained.

A Note On Marxist Thought in the Nineties

As Russia and Eastern Europe move towards free markets and demand economies (instead of command economies) and cast off the oppressive regimes that had ruled them, the question of the viability of Marxist critical thought is now an important one. Marxists in America and Western Europe argue that they are as happy as conservatives to see the totalitarian governments of Russia and Eastern Europe give way to democratic governments. The governments that ruled Russia and Eastern Europe were, many Marxists argue, not really Marxist but totalitarian societies that distorted true Marxism. In addition, it is the democratic and humanistic aspects of Marx's thought that they use, not his economic principles (which have always been suspect). These Marxists use his principles to help create a more democratic and humane society, not to convince people to set up communes and have a proletarian revolution.

Conservative thinkers and other anti-Marxists argue that Marxism is too "utopian" and lends itself to abuse too easily to be taken seriously. There are no "really" Marxist societies (and never have been) that are functioning as he would want them to function and the facade of moral superiority of Marxist governments (ruling in the name of the people) has given way to the reality of incredible depravity and worse privilege than exists in contemporary capitalist societies.

The debate on Marxism and its utility as an instrument of cultural analysis is currently being played out in scholarly journals in America and abroad. For our purposes the question is whether Marxism provides us with concepts that help us make sense of material culture and gain insights that other techniques do not offer? If so, we should use Marxist thought when applicable.

As Durkheim wrote, "social life, in all its aspects and in every period of its history, is made possible only by a vast symbolism. . . ." The value of things such as programs, trips, reports, articles, shows, conferences, parades, opinions, events, sights, spectacles, scenes and situations of modernity is not determined by the amount of labor required for their production. Their value is a function of the quality and quantity of experience they promise. Even the value of strictly material goods is increasingly similarly derived from the degree to which they promise to form a part of our modern experience. . . . Moreover, the old-style material type of commodity retains an important position in modern society only insofar as it has the capacity to deliver an experience: TVs, stereos, cameras, tape recorders, sports cars, vibrators, electric guitars or recreational drugs. The commodity has become a means to an end. The end is an immense accumulation of reflexive experiences which synthesize fiction and reality into a vast symbolism, a modern world.

—Dean MacCannell,
The Tourist: A New Theory of the Leisure Class

6

Sociological Perspectives on Material Culture

Sociology is generally understood to be the scientific study of groups and institutions and the patterns of relationships among members of these groups. The focus, then, is on collectivities and institutions (or structured relationships) in contrast to other perspectives, such as the psychological, that concerns itself with the psyche and internal states of individuals.

A sociological perspective on artifacts and objects, then, would investigate how objects are utilized by various groups or subgroups to do such things as establish identity (racial, religious, ethnic, geographical, gender, etc.), award status, confirm roles, reflect socioeconomic class and provide various kinds of gratifications. We must keep in mind in dealing with material culture from a sociological perspective that it is our perception of things, or, to be more precise, of what things mean, that shapes our behavior and not necessarily what things "really" mean. To modify (and get rid of the sexist language in) W. I. Thomas' famous dictum, "if people define situations as real, then they are real in their consequences."

Let me offer some definitions of the most important terms:
Role is understood to mean forms of behavior that are seen as appropriate to given situations. Status is defined as the rank one

has in a given organization or entity. Identity is used to suggest the sense of who one is, a matter often tied to groups one belongs to and the roles one plays. Erving Goffman, in *Relations in Public*, distinguishes between social identity and personal identity. Social identity, he writes (1971,189) involves:

> the broad social categories (and the organizations and groups that function like categories) to which an individual can belong and be seen as belonging: age-grade, sex, class, regiment and so forth.

Personal identity, on the other hand, refers to "the unique organic continuity imputed to each individual" (1971,189) and involves such things as one's name, appearance, biography, and social attributes.

Artifacts help establish social and personal identity on various levels as the chart below suggests:

Level of Identity	Artifact
National	Flag, Passport
Regional	Ten Gallon Hat
Religious	Cross
Occupational	Stethoscope, Beeper
Sub-Cultural	Leather Jacket, Studs, Heavy Boots
Political	*The Nation* on coffee table, NRA pin
Economic	*Wall Street Journal, Architectural Digest*

Socioeconomic class refers to the social and economic category one belongs to, based on such matters as income, education, and lifestyle. Gratifications are defined as the psychic (and other) rewards one gets from certain kinds of behavior which are generally connected to or related to artifacts and objects.

Life style is a rather vague and general concept which refers to the way people live—the kind of houses they live in, the cars they drive, the things they do and places they go for vacations, the clothes they wear, the occupations they have, the kind of food they eat, and so on. To a great degree life style is reflected in the material culture people employ to help define themselves. Sociologists are also concerned with societal norms and normless (anomic) behavior, which they contrast with alienated behavior, which suggests separation and lack of connections with society or some group.

In dealing with material culture from a sociological point of view, our concern is how the objects we are concerned with function. Functionalism, as sociologists understand the term, involves the role something (in our case, artifacts and objects) plays in keeping an entity in equilibrium. Something is functional if it helps maintain an entity, dysfunctional if it leads to the destruction of the entity, and nonfunctional if it plays no role. There is also that matter of functional alternatives, things which can be used instead of other things. Some sociologists, I should point out, consider functionalist analysis too static and conservative, and focus their attention on change, rather than continuity, as the central concern. How is change brought about and what impact do changes have on society?

We also make a distinction between the manifest or intended functions of phenomena and their latent or hidden and unintended functions. A number of sociologists suggest that sociology concerns itself to a great degree (if not primarily) with discovering the latent functions of phenomena (whether it be objects or behavioral patterns or organizations). When we look at material culture from a sociological perspective, then, we do so through a set of goggles which focus our attention primarily on certain aspects of our subject—those aspects relating to groups and institutions and the various concepts sociologists use to make sense of things.

Consider, for example, the impact that microwave ovens have had on American society. As of 1990, something like eighty percent of American homes have a microwave oven, and some market researchers predict that by 1995 the average American home will have two microwave ovens. These devices have had a number of unforeseen and unintended consequences.

For one thing, the family meal is often a casualty. The members of many families don't dine together anymore. Instead, it is a free-for-all in which members of a family zap dinners at various times, whenever their busy schedules offer some free time. Microwave ovens have also affected fast food chains. The fast food industry is now threatened, because food manufacturers are providing increasingly greater varieties of frozen dinners and other convenience foods—everything from pancakes to gourmet dinners. Microwaves provide almost immediate gratification, even faster than so-called fast food chains. Some people in the food industry worry that new generations of Americans, raised on microwave food, will not have any interest in food cooked in more traditional ways, in good cuisine. That is, there will be a lowering of our standards and food will be seen basically as "fuel."

Personally speaking, I think this notion is farfetched. In the case of San Francisco, for example, ethnic restaurants continue to flourish, even though many San Franciscans may be zapping Italian dinners, pizzas, and brownies day and night. It may be that the microwave leads Americans to savor other cuisines even more and may spark a counteraction, a return to home cooking—when time permits.

Let me offer another example of an object whose functions are worth considering—the Mehitzah, the screen or curtain used in Orthodox Jewish synagogues to separate men from women. (The Mehitzah is not used in Conservative or Reform synagogues.) The manifest function of the Mehitzah is to separate people on the basis of sex. One is not supposed to be distracted by members of the opposite sex. Many Jewish women, who are not Orthodox, find this practice repugnant and symbolic of what they consider to be sexist attitudes held by Orthodox Jews.

The latent function of the Mehitzah is to break up the family as a cohesive unit during the service, and to make the congregation the dominant unit in the synagogue, not the family. By doing this, the Orthodox argument goes, one prevents people from experiencing religion from a family perspective, from being distracted by one's family and from the sense that one is a member of a specific subgrouping in the congregation. The Mehitzah, then, can be seen as a signifier of an attempt to form a different kind of community in a religious congregation.

A psychiatrist I know, not an Orthodox Jew, suggested this theory to me. He believed that the traditional nuclear American family was under too much stress and was expected to do too much for its members, so the idea of separating family members for a religious experience seemed quite reasonable to him. This discussion of the Mehitzah shows that what's functional for one person or group

(Orthodox Jews) can also be seen as dysfunctional for another person or group (feminists). Deciding who is right about the functions or dysfunctions or manifest or latent functions of a Mehitzah or any artifact is not easy. One has to look at the contending arguments and see which one seems to make most sense.

Consider, for example, the theater and the importance props (objects, clothes, settings) have on audiences. We don't know what to make of actors or actresses on their own, though their physical characteristics, use of language and bearing might convey some information. But it is the clothes they wear and the settings in which we find them that help establish, in our minds, what kinds of people are being portrayed. Consider what is conveyed in the theater by a top hat, monocle, and spats. These are all, semiotically speaking, symbols whose meaning we must learn. Once we do, however, we are ready to assume (an example of metonymic association) that people wearing this kind of clothing will be upper-class or aristocratic and to assume, further, that they will behave in certain ways.

The so-called "status symbol" is a good example. Status symbols evolve. In the 1950s, for example, a Cadillac would have been seen as a status symbol in America, because it was one of the most expensive American cars made during that period. In the 1990s, Cadillacs no longer have as much status, especially with young, upwardly mobile, urban professionals (so-called Yuppies). They prefer German cars such as Mercedes Benzs and BMWs and consider people who buy Cadillacs to be "square" (that is, old fashioned people who aren't up on contemporary matters). Cadillac buyers, whose average age is 57, are disproportionately drawn from older elements of society, to whom a Cadillac was (when they were growing up) an important status symbol. What a status symbol does is broadcast to the world that one has "made it" and is, in financial terms, a "success." Status symbols must be objects that have a public dimension, that are seen and that are conventionally interpreted as conferring status.

Military insignia are a good example. In the United States Army, for example, everyone has a specific rank that is reflected in the insignia worn on one's hat and shoulders (in the case of officers) or armpatch (in the case of those who are not officers). The goal of insignia is to eliminate any ambiguity about a person's rank (and thus status). This is because there is a table which describes what each symbol (stripe, star, etc.) stands for.

There is a problem with interpreting status symbols. Sometimes people appropriate symbols that are "above" them. Many people who drive around in fancy German cars have leased them and may be spending a significant (maybe even disproportionate) amount of their income making claims to a status that they really don't deserve. Someone driving a BMW may not have a particularly good job and may not have any money in the bank. In the opposite vein, many people with high status (and income) pretend to be "common" and may wear Levi's and drive around in beat up old station wagons (though they may have a high status car in the garage). So status symbols can be used to lie—and so can other artifacts.

People can use everyday objects to fool us, also. Transvestites wear clothes of the opposite sex and impostors appropriate "professions" by, in part, adopting the dress and carrying (if not using) the implements of a given profession. In *Strategic Interaction*, Erving Goffman has a fascinating discussion of how American spies had to be careful about what they wore, to be seen as "authentic." He quotes *Sub Rosa: the OSS and American Espionage* by S. Alsop and T. Braden on how careful we had to be in outfitting spies:

> An agent traveling in an occupied country must wear clothes of the occupied country. The slightest variation will give him away. An American laundry and cleaning mark, for example, would be tantamount to a death warrant; yet those cleaning marks are impossible to remove. They had to be cut out and patched over, an improvisation which was suspicious and not entirely effective. Other give-aways are: the manner in which buttons are sewn on—The Americans do it criss-cross, Europeans in parallel; the lining—European linings are full; the adjustment buckles—in Europe they bear the mark of the country of origin; suspender buttons—no matter what European country they come from, they bear the imprint "Elegant," 'For Gentlemen," or "Mode de Paris." (Goffman 1969,25)

Thus it was not only the language abilities and the various fake passes that agents carried that was important, but also the clothes the agent wore and the everyday articles he might be carrying in his pockets.

Agents also have what are called "collections," things like old postcards mailed to an address in the country the spy claims to be from, library cards, stamped bus tickets, etc. which they leave in their apartments. They assume that their apartments will be surreptitiously searched by intelligence agents who will be led astray by the planted objects that "confirm" the pretended identity of the spy.

This shows the importance artifacts and objects have in conveying to others a sense of our identity. In everyday life, the objects we use (in addition to other things such as occupation) help us to confirm our identities with others and reaffirm, to ourselves, our sense of who we are.

Another interesting example of people using artifacts to lie involves the Broadway Riders, a southern California group of young men who pretend to be motorcyclists. Orrin E. Klapp describes this group of "motorcyclists without motorcycles" in *Collective Search for Identity* as follows:

> They affect the style of better-known motorcycle gangs such as Hell's Angels—black leather jackets, tight pants, boots, long hair, unkempt beards, chains, buckles, sheath knives protruding from boots, slit ear and earring, and so on. (Klapp 1969,103)

He quotes someone who manages a motorcycle show to the effect that the members of this gang do little more than hang around pizza parlors and discuss their exploits and their pseudo-motorcycles. Because motorcycle gangs have a particular style of dress, and use certain artifacts (sheath knives, chains, etc.) the members of this gang can adopt the look, even if they can't afford the cycles.

Sociologist Charles Winick has some interesting things to say about the Barbie Doll (and mannequin dolls in general) and the way they signify a change in the women's roles. He points out in his book, *The New People*, that many girls learned how to sew by working on clothes for their dolls and that "by taking care of her doll, a girl could project into the future and see herself as a mother. At the same time, the child could identify with the doll, since both were being taken care of by a mother" (Winick 1968, 207).

This changed, he argues, with the development of the mannequin doll, and leads to confusion in the minds of the children who
play with these dolls. He explains this as follows:

> What is the effect of these mannequin dolls on their millions of owners be-
> tween four and twelve? Such girls may be less able to achieve the emotional
> preparation for being a wife and mother that they received from baby dolls.
> Barbie is a sexy teen-ager. A girl who projects and sees her doll as a mother
> figure is seeing her mother as a teen-ager, which is certainly confusing. If the
> youngster identifies herself as the mother, then she is taking care of a child
> who is already an adolescent. (Winick 1968, 208)

Barbie and her best friend Midge, Winick suggests, spend a lot of
time competing with each other and with Ken (and for Ken), leading to a new kind of woman, who is always on the make, who
consumes endlessly and conspicuously, and who is extremely aggressive. This can cause trouble, Winick cautions, for young men
who traditionally are a couple of years behind women in achieving
puberty.

What might be most damaging, however, is that these dolls represent an attack on the latency period of young girls:

> The Barbie girl may learn to expect to be valued because of her ever-increasing
> wardrobe and ability to manipulate her father and, later, husband into buying
> clothes and more clothes. During the latency years, she is being introduced to
> precocious sexuality, voyeurism, fantasies of seduction, and conspicuous con-
> sumption. (Winick 1968, 209)

These fantasies are beyond the emotional capacities of their owners and deprive young children of an adequate latency period — a
period which Freudians and many others believe is necessary for
children if they are to develop correctly. In the case of girls, Winick
argues, they are also deprived of the benefits of symbolic mother-
hood (that comes from playing with a baby doll) and make up for
this, in later years, by purchasing stuffed dolls or Teddy Bears.

Winick argues in *The New People: Desexualization in American
Life* that American society is losing a sense of clear-cut gender
identification. There has been, he argues, a "radical dislocation of
sexual identity," (1968, x) and that may be the most important
event of our time. His book deals, in great part, with popular
culture and media, but he also has fascinating and highly contro-
versial things to say about guitars, pets (the popularity of cats,

which are seen by people as feminine), liquor, instant coffee, diet foods, cigars, furniture, appliances, clothes, and many other objects of material culture.

The manifest function of a Barbie doll is obvious—it is a doll for children to play with. The latent functions of this doll, both for the children who play with them and society, at large, are another matter. Winick implies that Barbie dolls are dysfunctional, that they inculcate bad values in young girls and deprive them of much of their latency period, something which impacts, in a negative way, on their social and sexual development.

An historian of art, Alan Gowans, has argued that Barbie Dolls actually represent a return to the earlier tradition (before 1850) of making dolls that represented adults and of preparing children for adult life. That raises some interesting questions: how did girls prepare for their roles as mothers before 1850 and, assuming that the latency period is necessary, what impact did these dolls have on the psychological development of young girls prior to 1850?

Much of the work on uses and gratifications comes from sociological studies of the mass media, in which the researchers studied how people used the media and what gratifications the media provided. This was a reversal of the more traditional approaches which investigated the effects the media had on people. If we look at objects and artifacts as, among other things, means of expression, the notion of considering the uses and gratifications we obtain from artifacts does not seem too difficult to entertain.

Consider, for example, pipes. Pipe smokers derive a considerable amount of gratification from sucking on pipe stems and blowing smoke around. Then there is the business of filling pipes. There is also the matter of scraping the pipe clean, fiddling around with one's tobacco pouch, the sensuous pleasure provided by the texture and smell of fine tobaccos, the pleasure of lighting a match or cigarette lighter, and the business of getting the newly filled pipe going. All of these things offer the pipe smoker comforting routines and things to do to occupy his (women seldom smoke pipes) fingers and time. There is also the matter of taking the pipe out of one's mouth, for whatever reason, and putting it back, which seems to give pipe smoker's pleasure. Pipe smokers probably also enjoy the smell of the burning tobacco.

There is connoisseurship to be displayed in terms of the kinds of tobacco smoked and in the kinds of pipes used. In addition, pipe smokers usually have collections of pipes and thus the pleasure connected with being a collector of handsome artifacts that reflect one's taste and sophistication must also be factored in.

In certain respects, then, pipe smoking might be described as functional for pipe smokers. It provides them with a number of momentary gratifications. It is dysfunctional, however, in that it leads to cancer and has harmful effects on others who are near the pipe smoker. The problem for the pipe smoker is that nicotine is a very powerful drug and it is difficult to stop smoking once habituated to it (or hooked on it).

In his classic study, *Yankee City*, W. Lloyd Warner pays considerable attention to the role of objects and artifacts in rituals that give individuals a sense of identity and status. He discusses family behavior in various classes and writes, about the life style of the wealthy in Yankee City:

> The elaborate ritual of the upper class in general is associated with strong feelings for property and its correct handling. . . . There is a definitely recognized household arrangement which each child is brought up to respect and the parts of which he must treat with almost ritual care. In this pattern, the antiques, heirlooms, and other properties which have been handed down from the past are the important centers around which other house furnishings are arranged. The inheritance of ritual objects from the past and their use by living lineal descendants provide the members of the upper-class group with a symbolic apparatus which ties the sentiments of the living with those of the dead. (Warner 1963, 64)

These objects, then, have, among their different functions, a primary symbolic one, which is to help members of the upper-class consolidate their identities.

Much of what Warner wrote about Yankee City (in reality, Newburyport, Massachusetts) in the thirties still holds true today. Members of the various echelons of the upper classes often signify their status in similar ways: living in large old houses in the best sections of town with old Persian rugs and "antique" family furniture (as contrasted with the Danish modern of the middle and lower-upper classes in their broadloom carpeted suburban ranch homes). In some cases, members of the lower-upper classes actually are wealthier than some upper-class families, but their money is old (like their furniture) and with some people it is the age of the money, not the quantity of the money, that is all important.

Technological developments in recent years have created two different kinds of radios that are, literally, worlds apart — the much-maligned "ghetto blaster" stereo portable and the personal portable "Walkman" style of radio or cassette player. The term "ghetto blaster" suggests something about who owns these radios and how they are used.

Ghetto blasters are large and powerful stereo radios (often with tape recording and even compact disk playing capabilities) that are frequently used by young people and members of minority groups, from one or another ghetto. These radios are, at their worst, played at a very high volume and impose the taste of the owners of the ghetto blasters on those around them (traditionally males use these radios, which are large and quite heavy).

The electronic power of the ghetto blaster may be a functional alternative to a sense of low status and economic powerlessness of the user of the ghetto blaster. Owners of ghetto blasters disobey the norms of public quiet and seem to enjoy doing so. One can imagine a mad situation in which owners of ghetto blasters have converged, accidently, in some large public area and each is listening to a different station and playing his blaster at top volume, leading to acoustic chaos.

The sphere of the ghetto blaster is public; the psychological imperatives at work are sociability (the kindest reading) and a desire to dominate and make oneself heard or one's presence known (the least kind reading).

The Walkman type of stereo radio is the polar opposite of the ghetto blaster. People who use these stereos essentially seal themselves off from the world and attempt to attain a state of pure acoustic sensation. There is something equally disturbing about this phenomenon. If ghetto blaster users are anomic, and disregard the rules of conduct and codes of civility relating to being quiet in public places, Walkmen users are alienated and antisocial. Walkmen users do not bother people the way ghetto blaster users do, but they do something even worse — they reject them. Walkmen users elevate and give primacy to their personal tastes and desire for separation, hiding behind or shutting the world out via a wall of sound.

The chart that follows shows the dynamics connected to the two kinds of listening:

Personal Stereo	Ghetto Blaster
Escape	Dominance
Hide Taste	Impose Taste
Alienation	Anomie
Isolation	Sociability, Dominance
Small	Large
Private	Public

What this chart demonstrates is that though the personal stereo users and ghetto blaster users are different, they are both similar in that they push various aspects of radio listening to extremes and these extremes reflect antisocial tendencies that are, shall we say, disquieting.

We can see, then, that the objects we have around us function in many different ways and help us do everything from consolidate our identities to play roles and make claims to statuses (to which we may or may not be "entitled"). The sociological approach to material culture focuses on the functions artifacts and objects have relative to such things as people's identities, roles and statuses. One might argue, in fact, that a great deal of our sociological knowledge comes from our ability to interpret material culture in terms of the fundamental categories of sociological thought. And that sociology is, to a large extent, grounded in material culture.

People may purchase things for personal or private reasons, but this does not mean that these objects and artifacts do not have, in addition, sociological significance and meaning. The task of the sociologist is to discover the latent functions and unintended consequences (both for individuals and society at large) of the objects and artifacts with which we surround ourselves and which play such an important role in our lives.

Part II

Perspectives on Fashion

Barthes finds that meaning in Fashion eventually arranges itself as a pyramid, the upper reaches of which comprise only very large categories like time, place, climate, ending with a summit, a final function which is "on all occasions." Let us stress once more that these are not truisms or part of a rationally arranged lexicon like Roget's Thesaurus *but attested phrases Barthes found in magazines. One even finds a garment which is expressly described as a universal:* tout-aller *and also* passe-partout *(for all occasions). This universal garment, which means everything, at first resembles what is indeed the only garment worn in underdeveloped countries. . . . Fashion seems to refer to institutionalized meanings, even naturalized ones. It is therefore a conjuring trick and one must now see what is at stake. Fashion suffers from a continuing loss of memory; its meaning is strong in the instant, but comes undone as time unfolds.*

—Annette Lavers,
Roland Barthes: Structuralism and After

7

The Semiotics of Fashion

Fashion comes from the Latin word *factio* and various French and Italian derivatives such as *facere* and means two things — "making" and "faction." This latter aspect of the term suggests differentiation, which plays an important part in fashion. From the semiologists and semioticians (who, for our purposes will be seen as essentially the same) we have learned to think of fashion, as an institution, as being like a language and what a person wears as being the equivalent of speech.

This distinction is explained by Roland Barthes in his *Elements of Semiology* where he explains that language is

> a systematized set of conventions necessary to communication, indifferent to the *material* of the signals which compose it . . . as opposed to which *speech* (parole) covers the purely individual part of language. (Barthes 1979,13)

That is, language is a social institution which has various rules and codes that we must all learn if we are to communicate with others effectively. Individuals learn these rules and codes and use them when they speak.

Speaking is an individual act but it is not "pure creation" Barthes tells us, for if it were, there would be no communication:

speech is essentially an individual act of selection and actualization; it is made in the first place of the "combination thanks to which the speaking subject can use the code of the language with a view to expressing his personal thought" . . . it is because speech is essentially a combinative activity that it is corresponds to an individual act and not pure creativity. (Barthes 1970,15)

When we speak we use words (signs, in semiological parlance) that have conventional meanings that others also use and understand. Sometimes, of course, we misunderstand one another and do not interpret the words correctly. This fact has relevance, we shall see, to fashion and the way we communicate with clothes. We can use the distinction between language and speaking to help understand the difference between fashion and personal dress, which can be seen as being the equivalent of an idiolect in linguistics.

Fashion is the infinity of articles of clothing that are available in a given society and personal dress is the combination of articles of clothing that an individual selects to wear at a given moment in time. We can see, then, that personal dress is the equivalent of speaking or saying something using elements that are similar to verbs and nouns and adjectives — elements such as shirts and pants and dresses and suits and shoes.

Barthes discusses the components of what he calls the "garment system" as follows:

> The language, in the garment system, is made i) by the oppositions of pieces, parts of garments and "details," the variation of which entails a change in meaning (to wear a beret or bowler hat does not have the same meaning); ii) by the rules which govern the associations of the pieces among themselves, either on the length of the body or in depth. Speech, in the garment system, comprises all the phenomena of anomic fabrication (few are still left in our society) or individual way or wearing (size of the garment, degree of cleanliness or wear, personal quirks, free association of pieces). (Barthes 1970,27)

When we dress, then, we generally follow certain rules of combinations — what are called "codes" — that tell us what articles go with what other articles. Generally these rules of combination are conventions, but in some cases they are actually articulated as "dress codes."

For example, men generally do not wear a striped tie with a striped shirt or a striped shirt with checkered pants. This is because we believe there should be contrasts in our clothes between "busy" designs and solid colors or darks ·and lights, though, of course, these codes are often "violated" by people wishing to make some kind of a statement about themselves. There are also, of course, regional styles of dress which connect a person to a particular area or locale in the same way that one's accent or dialect does.

We might say that just as a sentence is a set of elements assembled in a certain way, personal dress is a set of articles from the garment system assembled in a particular way. An outfit that mixes plaids and stripes is as "wrong" as an ungrammatical sentence, since it violates the rules of combination.

Let me show the various relationships discussed above in the following chart.

Language	Speech
Fashion	Personal Dress
Social Institution	Individual Act
Grammar	Codes
Dialect	Regional Dress

The language of dress is much more limited than language itself, since we have an almost unlimited number of words at our disposal while our personal dress is limited to the clothes that we have purchased (or that we can afford). And words do not go out of fashion as quickly as clothes.

Let us take a hypothetical case of a person who is dressed as any one of millions of persons might be dressed. He is wearing cotton underpants, a cotton tee shirt, a cotton blue-denim workshirt, a pair of Levi's "shrink fit" denims, cotton stockings and running shoes. The widespread popularity of wearing blue jeans (waning slightly now, in the early Nineties, but still very strong) is a phenomenon I call denimization. What does deminization mean? How does one explain it?

In order to do this, and following the analogy of language (where we learn that meaning stems from oppositions), it is useful to contrast denimization with its opposite, haute couture, or "high fashion." Denim, for our purposes and in its original incarnation, was certainly "low fashion," and was originally thought of as work clothing. It was cheap and strong—two virtues that were its main selling points. On the other hand, garments found in "high fashion" are generally made of fancy fabrics which are expensive, scarce, and delicate.

High fashion clothes are associated not with work but leisure. Also, high fashion clothes imply uniqueness, individuality, and discrimination as contrasted with mass-produced and uniform-like blue jeans. We often purchase high fashion garments at boutiques, where we get handmade clothes, fitted to us. We get blue jeans in department stores or stores that sell mass-produced leisure clothes.

We can see the difference between the two polarities—blue jeans and high fashion clothes—in the chart below.

High Fashion	Blue Jeans/Low Fashion
Fancy material	Common material (denim)
Expensive	Cheap
Leisure	Work
Individuality	Uniformity
Hand made	Factory made
Boutique	Department Store

A glance at this chart, which deals with what denim means (or used to mean) in relation to high fashion clothes shows that something has happened, in recent years, to the way we perceive denim. Things have changed a great deal and now most of the things that can be said of high fashion clothes can be said of denim—it is handmade in boutiques, it is often associated with leisure and play, and it is no longer always cheap, especially when compared to synthetic fabrics.

It is possible to see in denimization something analogous to "the American Dream." Denim is an immigrant fabric (denim is an Americanization of "De Nimes," from Nimes) which has made good in America. It also symbolizes, one might argue, a significant change that is taking place in American society where work is losing its identity and being transformed, more and more, into play. At the same time, play seems to be more and more transformed into work.

We can see this when we examine the relationship that exists between fashion and work. In many occupations people wear what used to be seen as play garments to work and work garments (leisure suits) to play. In many universities professors wear very casual clothes. It is not too much of an exaggeration to say that the professors look like the custodians and the custodians look like the professors. This varies from department to department. Conventionally, administrators and business professors still dress formally with shirts, ties, and suits. Members of the departments involving the arts, on the other hand, often dress casually.

If I am correct, then, work and leisure are no longer seen as polar opposites. This has generated changes in our fashions in which denim has become a kind of universally accepted garment material, one which does not serve the purpose of differentiating between people but, instead, masking and disguising. A person wearing blue jeans could be a truck driver or a neurosurgeon. Denim is ecumenical and universalistic and, as such, mystifies by de-identifying its wearers; it is a perfect garment for people who wish to disguise themselves.

Perhaps denim's power stems from this ability it has; it dissolves identities and frees people to play all kinds of identity games. This does not mean that denim increases our individuality. It may be that we become de-individuated when we present ourselves to the world with no signs or indicators of who we are and how we expect to be perceived and treated.

Jonathan Culler has commented on the semiological significance of fashion, and its social implications, as follows:

> Fashion is a social system based on convention. If clothing had no social significance people might wear whatever seemed most comfortable and buy new clothes only when the old wore out. By giving meaning to certain details — calling them stylish or appropriate for certain occasions and activities — the fashion system enforces distinctions among garments and speeds up the process of replacement: "c'est le sens qui fait vendre." ("It's the meaning which sells.") (Culler 1975,32–33)

Fashion has a social significance and it is the duty of the semiologist, Culler suggests, to demonstrate the mechanisms by which this meaning in fashion is generated. Distinctions among garments imply distinctions among people. Denimization tends to blur all these distinctions.

Americans have always believed that their so-called "classlessness" has diminished status anxiety but I would argue just the opposite—that "classlessness" generally heightens status anxiety and complicates social relationships. In societies in which class lines are definite and recognizable through clothing and accent, there is little status anxiety, though there is often a great deal of resentment and class conflict. Americans always have a problem locating people they meet in some class-related niche, so they know how to relate to them—how much deference to pay them, what to talk about, and so on. When this is not done easily and quickly it leads to a considerable amount of confusion and anxiety.

In a denimized society, people hide their class backgrounds which means that nobody can be sure how they should treat anyone else. Some people have seen denimization as an indication of a leveling downward and a more egalitarian perspective in the general public, but this view is questionable. Marvin Harris, an anthropologist, has suggested a different view. In his book *Cows, Pigs, Wars and Witches*, he suggests that what I have called denimization represents a movement away from conspicuous consumption by the rich and an aping of the rich by the middle classes:

> Conspicuous consumption in the grand manner became dangerous, so highest prestige now once again goes to those who have the most but show least. With the most prestigious members of the upper class no longer flaunting their wealth, some of the pressure on the middle class to engage in conspicuous consumption has also been removed. This suggests to me that the wearing of torn jeans and the rejection of overt consumerism among middle-class youth of late has more to do with aping the trends set by the upper class than with any so-called cultural revolution. (Harris 1975,129–30)

Harris wrote this in 1975, before the Reagan era, and the return to conspicuous consumption by some of the super-rich (the symbol of this being Malcolm Forbes' multimillion dollar party) but I think his words still apply to most Americans.

There is a big difference between wearing old jeans and what I have called denimization, but there may be an element of imitating the rich behind it. It may also be that taste is now moving from the lower classes and working classes *upwards*, so that denimization represents the triumph of working-class taste asserting itself at the moment when the working class seems to be losing its identity as a cultural force.

"A sense of being perfectly well dressed," a lady is reported as saying to Emerson, "gives a feeling of inward tranquility which religion is powerless to bestow." In the same way, Nietzsche has said that a pretty woman conscious of looking her best, never caught a cold however scanty her gown; the saying is poetically if not literally true. We know that female prisoners, isolated from mankind, sustain their morale by the use of cosmetics, much as empire builders used to dine in boiled shirts although separated by two thousand leagues of desert from the next black tie; in the same way a uniform is known to exert a powerful effect upon conduct, and its careful upkeep is accounted a most important part of the duty of a soldier.

—Quentin Bell,
On Human Finery

8

Myth, Ritual, and Fashion

According to the Old Testament, in the myth of creation, Adam was originally naked and thought nothing of it. We find Adam and Eve in the Garden and "they were not ashamed." Let me quote the passage, since it has had such an incredible impact on the western world:

Now the serpret was more subtle than any beast of the field which the Lord God had made.

And he said unto the woman,

"Yea, hath God said Ye shall not eat of every tree of the Garden?"

And the woman said unto the serpent,

"We may eat of the fruit of the trees of the garden: but of the fruit of the tree which is in the middle of the garden, God hath said "Ye shall not eat of it, neither shall ye touch it, lest ye die."

And the serpent said unto the woman,

"Ye shall surely not die: for God doth know that in the day ye eat thereof, then your eyes shall be opened, and ye shall be as gods, knowing good and evil."

And when the woman saw that the tree was good for food and that it was pleasant to the eyes, and a tree to be desired to make one wise, she took of the fruit thereof, and did eat, and gave also to her husband with her; and he did eat. And the eyes of both of them were opened, and they knew that they were naked; and they sewed fig leaves together, and made themselves aprons.

Adam and Eve then hid from God, who discovered that they had eaten from the tree ("I was afraid, because I was naked; and I hid myself" says Adam). God banished Adam and Eve from Paradise and with that act history begins.

We find, here, a connection between being naked and innocence, and it has been suggested by Mircea Eliade that people who are nudists are seeking (whether they recognize it or not) to regain a state of radical innocence by returning to man and woman's state before the Fall—when we felt no shame. As Eliade suggests in *The Sacred and The Profane* (1959,134) in a discussion of baptismal nudity:

> Baptismal nudity too bears a meaning that is at once ritual and metaphysical. It is abandoning "the old garment of corruption and sin, which the baptized person takes off in imitation of Christ, the garment with which Adam was clothed after his sin"; but it is also a return to primitive innocence, to Adam's state before the fall. "O admirable!" Cyril writes. "Ye were naked before the eyes of all and felt no shame. Because verily ye bear within you the image of the first Adam, who was naked in Paradise, and felt no shame."

There is, then, a sacred dimension to nudity and, by implication, a profane dimension to being clothed. Clothes are signifiers of guilt and sin.

For Eliade, modern man and woman have the illusion that they have escaped the sacred dimensions of life; what has happened, he argues, is that rites and myths have become camouflaged and are not easily available to our consciousness. But these sacred myths and rites are still powerful and influence us. As he points out in a chapter titled "Human Existence and the Sanctified Life":

> But is not only in the "little religions" or in the political mystiques that we find degenerated or camouflaged religious behavior. It is no less to be seen in movements that openly avow themselves to be secular or even anti-religious. Examples are nudism or the movement for complete sexul freedom, ideologies in which we can discern traces of the "nostalgia for Eden," the desire to re-establish the paradisal state before the Fall, when sin did not exist and there was no conflict between the pleasures of the flesh and conscience. (Eliade 1959,207)

History begins with the act of wearing clothes and society maintains itself, in part, through clothes, since they provide a means for people to differentiate themselves and are signifiers of status and rank and many other things.

The story of Joseph is instructive in this respect. In this story we find that Israel (Jacob) loved his Joseph more than his other sons.

> Now Israel loved Joseph more than than all his children, because he was the son of his old age; and he made him a coat of many colors. And when his brethren saw that their father loved him more than all his brethren, they hated him and could not speak peaceably unto him.

This led Israel's other children to hate Joseph and to the conspiracy that ended up with Joseph being cast into a pit. And it was Joseph's coat which the brothers smeared with kid's blood and brought back to Israel when they wanted him to believe that Joseph had been killed. His response was to tear his clothes and put on sackcloth while he mourned his son. Clothing now, we find, is used in many different ways and is connected with different rituals and observances.

What follows draws on an article by Moshe Meiselman in *Sh'ma* magazine. He argues that in Jewish thought the body is considered holy. This contrasts with Christian thought, which sees it as sinful and Greek thought which sees it as an object of beauty. The Jews also see the body as beautiful, but this is not as important as its holiness. Thus, the Greeks felt it was desirable to display the body and did so in numerous statues in which the body was shown without clothes. The Jews, on the other hand, clothed the body lest its physical beauty interfere with man's spiritual goals and his quest for the divine.

Jewish thought is based upon a different reading of the creation story from the one discussed earlier. As Meiselman writes:

> The *Midrash* [early Jewish interpretation of The Torah] is very detailed in its description of the background of the sin of Adam and Eve. The physical world was not created in an amoral context, but with a moral goal. The physical creation was meant to be the means for achieving spiritual and moral goals. Man in the Garden of Eden was freed from the harsh realities of life to devote himself completely and exclusively to sanctifying the physical through its usage for spiritual ends. (Meiselman 1976)

In the Garden there is not split between man's physical and spiritual nature. It was Eve's act that led to this dissociation, her pursuit of pleasure for its own sake which "divorced the physical from its spiritual goal."

Jewish thought does not condemn the pursuit of pleasure, and in certain respects one might say it demands it. Judaism is not an ascetic religion; rejecting pleasure suggests that one finds God's creation of the world objectionable, in certain respects. Judaism, however, does reject the single-minded pursuit of pleasure which diverts man from his spiritual obligations. As a verse in the Torah states, "And you shall not go after your heart and after your eyes."

Thus, Jewish thought puts a different light on clothing. We do not wear clothes because we are sinners, it suggests, but because we do not wish to be diverted from what is most important—our spiritual goals. Our attitudes towards our bodies shape our fashions, though there are other factors at work also (the weather, money, etc.). In contemporary Western societies, it would seem that the Hellenistic perspective, which sees the body as beautiful and a source of erotic pleasure, is winning out, but there has been a shift from men's bodies to women's bodies.

Many blue jeans are designed to fit very tightly over the buttocks and are very revealing. They have more or less abandoned their historical association with manual labor and the working classes and are now a means of sexual display. In this respect, they also are functional for the homosexual community.

Let me suggest that there is a connection between myths (which are understood as sacred stories) and everyday life. A myth often has an historical impact, is reflected in elite arts and popular culture and, finally, everday life. Let us take this "myth model" and use it to see fashion (and, when possible, denimization) in some kind of perspective:

MYTH	Adam and Eve in Garden
HISTORICAL REFLECTIONS	Pioneer in buckskins, forty-niners in California
ELITE ARTS	Gogol's "The Overcoat"
POPULAR CULTURE	Books on Power Dressing
EVERYDAY LIFE	Wearing blue jeans, "denimization"

Wearing jeans, we can see, may be based on a decision a given individual makes, but it is connected to myths that continue to shape our perception of the world, whether we recognize this or not.

I would like to conclude this discussion of the mythic aspects of fashion with a look at some American culture heroes who are identified with specific kinds of clothes. By culture heroes I mean certain figures or "ideal types" who have played a central role in American history—the Puritan, the Pioneer, and the Plutocrat.

Most Americans make a mistake when they visualize the typical Puritan; they confuse the Puritans with the Pilgrims, whose style of dress was much different. The Pilgrims who came to American in 1620, were a radical group from the working classes, essentially, and dressed austerely. Ten years after the Pilgrims came to America the Puritans arrived. They were essentially middle-class and were led by landed gentry, wealthy merchants, and a number of university graduates.

According to Norman Foerster, the Puritans had (1957,8)

> great interest in the arts of dress and the home. Even "the sternest of them," says James Truslow Adams, "had their portraits painted, wore rich clothes and accumulated beautiful furniture and costly plate." Dress closely corresponded to social position, and if common folk wore coarse and sober clothes, it was not from preference but in obedience to custom and law. In 1651 the General Court of Massachusetts proclaimed its "utter detestation that men and women of mean condition, education and calling, should take upon them the garbe of gentlemen by wearing gold or silver lace, or buttons or pognots at their knees, or walke in great boots, or women of the same ranke to wear silke or tiffany hoods or scarfs."

This passage not only reveals something about the fashions of the time, but also demonstrates that the "lower classes" have always imitated the upper classes by appropriating their clothing styles, to the extent their finances allowed them to do so.

The Puritans, in turn, imitated European fashions:

> Gentlemen tried to ape London fashions, sometimes importing dolls as models, and their wardrobes were resplendent with bright blue and scarlet silks, elaborate embroidery, and creamy lace. Wealthy men shared this taste for costly materials and vivid colors. Their frock coats were sometimes decorated with gold lace, and they wore knee-breeches of brocade, plush, or silk, silk stockings, knee-buckles and shoe-buckles of silver and gold. (Foerster 1957,8)

The Puritans may have been motivated by Christian theology, but as far as fashion is concerned, they were Hellenists.

The pioneer, our second culture hero, is a different matter; here we have a figure in deerskins, moccasins, and coonskin hats—a figure close to nature and not wearing European finery. The pioneer is a composite figure — hunter, trapper, deerslayer, farmer, and so on. His clothing symbolizes a rejection of European culture and history and a stance outside of time (and history, institutions, etc.) and *in* space (the vast American wilderness).

The pioneer dresses the way he does because of the imperatives of nature and the frontier. He strips away European clothing (and with it European culture, history, institutions), puts on deerskins and the other pioneer garb, and enters into the forest. His experience in nature creates the "new" American hero, a new man. The Puritan, we must remember, is really a transplanted European who has brought his European culture with him. He is able to create a different kind of society in America, but it is really only a modification of European society.

The pioneer, on the other hand, represents something new — and it is reflected in his clothing, which is, in effect, Native American clothing. It is the clothing that is most functional in the Garden, which is how we often referred to the vast wilderness in America. Returning to the Garden and settling the Frontier creates a new Adamic figure. Is it not possible to see in blue jeans, a modern functional-equivalent of the deerskins of the pioneers? Don't blue jeans (accompanied as they often are by blue chambray work shirts and even work boots) represent a desire for a return to innocence, to the days of the frontier when class distinctions were not great, when we generated, thanks to the virgin land and its imperatives, "individuals" in a classless, paradiscal America?

When we come to our third culture hero, the plutocrat, figures from cartoons crowd into our minds. The frontier has ended, Americans are no longer innocent, and our society has been "corrupted" by European culture, ideas and institutions. Here we find old men in top hats and evening dress, perhaps with diamond tie pins, puffing fat cigars in stately mansions. *Plutus* was the god of wealth in Greek mythology and the plutocrat of the early twentieth century in our cultural imagination is the wealthy man who often "controls" the government and uses his power to plunder enormous wealth from American society and sink the masses ever deeper into poverty and misery. This figure is, of course, a stereotype but there are elements of truth in it.

With the plutocrat we are back to Puritan conceptions of dress, which is fitting since it can be argued that the plutocrat is a creation of the Puritan ethos. It stressed man's duty to act in the world and supplied the rationale (so many argue) for the development of capitalism. The Puritans argued that we were predestined, and that those who were wealthy could see it as a sign of God's love. The American plutocrats separated this aspect of Puritan thought from its other side — its ideas about our obligations to our fellow men and society, its stress on charity and social responsibility.

If you were to take the popularity of blue jeans or what I have called "denimization" as an important fashion statement, it might be possible to argue that from the end of World War Two until the eighties we have been living in a proletarian age, when millions of American young people (and not-so-young) were dressing poor or proletarian style in blue jeans and accompanying fashion styles. In the eighties, the so-called "greed decade," blue jeans were still popular in America but had lost their dominating position as people used their wealth to dress fancier. What will happen in the nineties remains to be seen. A great deal will depend on which culture heroes (and now culture heroines) become dominant. The war in Iraq led to an explosion of interest in military style clothing, but I suspect this is only a passing fancy, a momentary indulgence as we grope towards who we want to be and, as a result of our decision, what we should look like.

July 14, 1980. Bastille Day. On Broadway at Seventy-second, a bus rattles to its stop. Above, a blur of color—bright red, orange, shocking saffron, lavender blue, marine, livid, purplescent, raven—invades the corridor of vision. Looking up, we see a poster ad that, running along the entire roof of the bus, offers an outrageous display: an assembly line of female backsides, pressed emphatically into their designer jeans. On the right hip pocket of each, the signature of an heiress . . .

The bus moves along. Pinned to its rear, we see its final reminder: "The Ends *Justify the Jeans . . . Gloria Vanderbilt for Murijani." Today's freedom is molded and taut. An animal in perpetual heat. Individuals are identical but come in colors. Over this rainbow lies the promise of perpetual pleasure.*

—Stuart and Elizabeth Ewen,
Channels of Desire: Mass Images and the
Shaping of American Consciousness

9

The Psychology of Fashion

A student of mine, who had been institutionalized for schizophrenia, told me that whenever she felt she was about to "go off the deep end" she always put on a certain yellow dress. This garment was a signal from her unconscious about her mental state. She was not aware of this until she started therapy and discovered that there was a connection between her psychological states and the clothes she wore. In the same manner Eisenhower is reputed to have worn a brown suit when he was in a bad mood and members of his staff learned to expect a difficult time when they saw him wearing it.

Probably all of us recognize that when we are in certain moods we wear clothes which both minister to our needs and signal our emotional states to others—if they have learned to recognize the messages we are sending, that is. If you accept the notion that fashion is a form of communication—and sometimes this communication is not done at the conscious level—then it is not difficult to see a relationship between our moods and feelings and the clothes we wear.

We do not, as a rule, purchase clothes only on the basis of price. We do not buy clothes because they are the least expensive items we can get and they will last the longest. Even for people who do have limited means, there are a number of different options available at a given price, so price alone is seldom the determining factor in our choice of clothes.

From a psychoanalytic point of view, we choose garments to send messages, to create images of ourselves so others will know who we are and so we will know who we are. We know from the work of social psychologists that an identity is created, not given, and that it is based, to a considerable degree, on the feedback we get from "significant others." Thus, in creating an image of ourselves and for ourselves, through fashion (and other means), we attempt to generate responses from others which will affirm or reinforce our sense of who and what we are.

The process is a complicated one, admittedly. But our identities are, to a considerable degree, socially confirmed and this process is related to messages we send to others about ourselves by the way we dress and the responses we get from others. A good deal of this message sending, by using fashion, is not done consciously.

From this point of view, fashion is not always a "false front" meant to manipulate others, though, of course, there are times when people do use fashion to make claims to status that are not correct as far as their occupation and income are concerned. The relationship that exists between fashion and "the self" is a highly problematic one. In an essay in *Rolling Stone* (3 January 1974) Tom Wolfe explains his views on the matter:

> The conventional wisdom is that fashion is some sort of storefront that one chooses, honestly or deceptively, to place between the outside world and his "real self."

Proponents of this view seem to assume that people have selves or identities that are somehow "given" and that fashion is either consciously or unconsciously manipulative. People might understand what they are doing when they choose certain fashions or not understand the significance of their fashion choices, but in either case fashion functions as a kind of *persona* or mask, behind which a real self is disguised

Wolfe cites a different view of the matter:

> But there is a counter notion: namely, that every person's "real self," his psyche, his soul is largely a product of fashion and other outside influences on

his status. Such has been the suggestion of the stray figure here and there: the German sociologist Rene König, for example, or the Spanish biologist Jose M. R. Delgado.

This view argues that social forces and other phenomena, of which fashion is very important, shape personality and identity, so that fashion is not so much a consequence of conscious choice but, instead, some kind of a causal agent. Clothes, in a very real sense, do "make" the man and woman.

There is a benefit and a problem to the power that fashion changes have. On the one hand we can be many different persons, so to speak, as we change our styles and looks. This can be a help to men and women who find their spouses getting "tired" of them. Through the magic of fashion we can continually become "different" husbands and wives. (The same thing is at work on an individual basis. Sometimes we get "tired of ourselves" and dissatisfied with the way we look and thus can gain some measure of relief by adopting a new look.) The problem with this, if we carry it to an extreme, is that we stand in danger of losing our identities. One of the notions behind identity is that of stability or continuity, and we can lose our sense of self in the chaos of different styles and personas we adopt.

This matter is more of a theoretical problem than an actual one, since most people have neither the time, the money, nor the energy needed to produce constant changes in their wardrobes and identities. But what I've discussed here is important for it points out how fashion does enable us to create—if only superficially and temporarily—new identities which we all can experiment with. These identities are, I might add, made available and acceptable to people by the culture or subcultures to which they belong and related matters such as class and occupation.

Bikinis represent a revealing (in more ways than one) case study of the influence of culture and values on fashion. The earliest bikinis covered women's navels and some magazines, such as *Seventeen*, had a policy of airbrushing out navels from photographs and advertisements so that "idealized" navel-less women were presented to their readers. This did not last very long and the relatively chaste American bikini fell victim to the European bikini marking the end, it might be argued, of Puritanism's dominating influence on American culture and society. And now, of course, we have the Brazilian "thong" or micro-bikini which covers little more than the nipples of a woman's breasts and her pubic hair.

On the other hand, it might be argued that these micro-bikinis represent a movement in the direction of complete nudity—which is mythically connected to the notion of innocence. In the Garden of Eden, Adam and Eve were naked. It was only after they had eaten from the tree that they realized that they were naked and clothed themselves. Thus, nudity or nakedness (some distinguish between the terms) unconsciously reflects a desire for returning to the Garden and the micro-bikini is not sexually provocative but, in terms of its hidden imperatives, just the opposite. Nude women are not as sexually stimulating to men as partially clothed women and the same applies, no doubt, to men.

As early as the late sixties, women's clothing stores were selling more pants than skirts. We are all used to seeing women wear pants, but we must recognize that until the Second World War, women seldom wore pants. Pants were traditionally seen, in America, as male dress. Thus the fact that women adopted pants is of some significance. In recent years men have started wearing "feminized" clothing such as frilly shirts and nylon tricot underpants. And they wear scents, as well.

Furthermore, in recent decades there has been a revolution in men's fashion. Men's suits and other clothes change just as rapidly as women's, which means that men now spend a good deal more money on clothes than they did when suits had a kind of stylistic "immortality" and hardly ever changed. It might even be argued that there has been a strange kind of crossover, with men increasingly interested in displaying their bodies and women downplaying their bodies and trying to emphasize their minds. The growing power of the homosexual movement and of the feminists have, no doubt, contributed to this phenomenon.

If we define desexualization as a blurring of gender distinctions (and perhaps even what Charles Winick describes in *The New People* as a "radical dislocation of sexual identity"), perhaps something positive has taken place. Men no longer have to live up to limiting and destructive "macho" self-images (or definitions of what it is to be a man) and can freely express the feminine components of their psyches. But how far these trends can go without generating social and psychological confusion about male-female identities and relationships is a problem.

In an article by Julie Smith in *The San Francisco Chronicle* (2 February 1976) we read:

> Linda wore a demure gray pantsuit. Michael a Quiana shirt with the top two buttons open. She dined on shrimp and steak, he on shrimp teriyaki.
>
> They drank a bottle of vin rose, talking casually of mutual friends. They had known each other for six months, but this was only their second date.
>
> After the meal she wiped her lips delicately, placed her napkin on the table and looked squarely at him. "Now," she announced, "I'm going to take you home to bed."
>
> He made a little joke: "You just want me for my body."
>
> She didn't laugh. "That's right," she said, matter-of-factly.
>
> "I'm easy," he said, "but not that easy."

This incident is not fiction but was overheard at a restaurant; it would seem to be a textbook case of role-reversal in which a woman, in a pantsuit, is acting the way what we used to call "predatory" males act. The question we must ask is whether this kind of behavior is essentially role reversal or the reflection of a different attitude towards sexuality which affects men and women.

Women's bodies have traditionally been seen as legitimate objects for male lust. In recent years men's bodies have become the object of female lust, but not to the same extent, by any means. Photographs and other representations of nude or seminude women, in sexually stimulating poses, are seen with much more frequency than those of men. Raphael Patai explains this phenomenon in *Myth and Modern Man* (1972,298–299):

> To this day there is an incomparably greater emphasis on the representation and display of female, than of male, sexual charms. The pictures of nude or almost nude women, seen in so many places and in numerous media, are displayed with the obvious intention of attracting and arousing men. No comparable display of male nudity can be observed; moreover, where naked men are exhibited in photographs or in the flesh, the purpose is, as a rule, to attract male homosexuals, and not females, though the latter, too, may derive enjoyment or erotic pleasure from viewing them.

The reason for this, Patai explains, is that there is a difference between men and women in what arouses either sex. Patai mentions a number of studies which suggest that "men are more re-

sponsive to visual and psychological sexual stimuli." Men have
also, in Western countries and many others, more freedom and
power to give free reign to their sexual hunger and desires. Displaying photos and other representations of beautiful women also
serves as a validation, to others, of one's masculinity and thus
becomes functional.

Masculine narcissism tends to be based on traits such as "manli-
ness" and "virility," not beauty, and men traditionally have defined
themselves as subjects and agents, who can pursue women, and
not as objects to be pursued by others. This seems to be changing,
as the article quoted above suggests.

What seems to be happening is that there is a diminution of the
differences in traditional sexual roles, a breaking down of the distinctions that used to exist in rather ironclad ways. Certainly at the
extremes, in which we find super-macho male studs spending a
great deal of their time and energy pursuing super-sexy glamour
girls, this lessening or blurring of sexual differences will have salu-
tary effects. The problem lies at the center where there may occur
confusion about sexual identities (and roles) that may create problems of considerable magnitude, both for the individuals involved
and for society.

In the late seventies in San Francisco, the fashion scene was all
mixed up. The macho segments of the gay community wore crew-
cuts, leather boots, denims, and lumberjack shirts. Women were
wearing clothes featuring big shoulders and a "militaristic" look
was popular, inspired, it seems, by pre-Hitlerite German military
uniforms. At the same time men wore loose shirts (often with
banded collars), unconstructed jackets that gave them small shoulders, and pleated pants with straight legs. In the early nineties,
teenagers and women in their twenties have taken to wearing short
skirts with pantyhose, which represents a kind of "little girl" look
and may be an indicator of a kind of regression and an unconscious retreat from "adulthood" and sexuality. There is an element
of ambivalence at work in this style, too. For women display their
legs and their bodies with this style, but it is still quite different
from displaying breasts and cleavage.

Is it possible that the blue color of denims triggers certain unconscious responses in people (probably various kinds of sexual

fantasies)? This may sound like a farfetched notion, but Ernest Dichter argues in one of his books that the popularity of a brand of coffee was connected to the color blue it used on its cans, which generated sexual fantasies in people when they were shopping at supermarkets. The color blue has important psychological meanings. In American culture blue is associated with "blue laws" and rigid prohibitions on sexuality. But we also talk about "blue" material in comedy and dramas which is material that is sexually explicit. So we see blue in ambivalent terms as far as the psyche is concerned.

There is also the matter of the weight of these pants and the strength they have to protect us from the elements (as well as our hopes that they will last a long time). Shrink-fit Levi's also have a magical component which enables people to personalize or individualize these mass-produced pants. You are supposed to put on the Levis, sit in the bath or take a shower and the Levis shrink to fit the contours of your body. These Levis become a kind of second skin and have a psychological importance to us, whether we recognize it or not. They also serve the purpose of displaying our bodies better than loose-fitting blue jeans, though many brands of blue jeans are designed to do an even better job of this than shrink-fits.

In recent years blue jeans seem to have lost their overwhelming dominance as one component of the unofficial "uniform" of young men and women in America, though jeans are still extremely popular. What this change in taste (or seeming taste) means is difficult to say. It may be connected to the emergence of subcultures and the sense ethnic identities have of their value and importance. These factors would tend to "liberate" numbers of individuals from feeling it necessary to adopt a standard American form of dress. It may be that affluence has made us feel it no longer necessary to wear jeans. It may also be that there is widespread anxiety and depression in American society which we assuage (in part) by buying clothes.

Depression is generally considered to be anger directed at the self. Thus, if we can change our appearances, not only do we appear to be a "new" person to our spouses or loved ones, and thus counter the "boredom" factor, we also (we hope) trick ourselves into thinking that we are a new person. New clothes allow us to be "born again" and to escape, if only momentarily, the anger and guilt we feel about ourselves.

For people with a psychological perspective, the mystery of personality deepens with every article of clothing a person puts on. To know and understand people we do not strip them bare but, conversely, see what they wear. Clothes not only make the man and women, paradoxically, they reveal them.

Proof of the fact that prestige or power alone cannot control the direction of fashion is seen in the unsuccessful attempt of the clothing manufacturers, designers, fashion magazines, and acknowledged fashion leaders to reverse the trend toward shorter skirts which started in 1919 and went on until 1929. A similar campaign late in 1968 and in 1969 and 1970 to dampen the mass enthusiasm for miniskirts also was a partial failure . . .

Often, once a new fashion has been adopted, it seems to compel adherence, at least for a period of time. Thus the role of fashion may be to aid the collective adjustment of society to a changing world. First, fashion introduces a measure of uniformity where there would otherwise be chaos. By fostering unanimity and order, fashion thus performs in a rapidly changing society a function which custom performs in a settled society.

Second, fashion serves to detach the grip of the past. By placing value on being "up to date" and scorning older forms, it frees the way for movement in new directions. Finally, it helps prepare people for the immediate future.

—Helen MacGill Hughes,
Crowd and Mass Behavior

10

The Social Dimensions of Fashion

Although individuals choose the specific items that make up their wardrobes, the decisions they make have, it can be argued, already been made for them. We choose garments on the basis of needs we have, desires we have, aspirations we have, goals we have, and money we have. But though we may *choose* as we please (and I am returning here to an argument made by Jonathan Edwards in the early seventeenth century) it can be questioned whether or not we can *please* as we please. We select what we want to purchase and wear from a wide range of possibilities open to us but the basis of our selection is connected to various social and cultural pressures that are exerted upon us; we are aware of some of these imperatives and unaware of others.

If you ask a young man why is he is wearing jeans, for example, he might tell you that they "look good" or make him "feel good." Or that they are very comfortable. But what, specifically, is there about faded blue cotton pants that "looks" good? Where is the locus in taste? It is, I would suggest, in his social class (or the social class to which he aspires), his subculture, and the group of people with whom he associates.

While people have a great deal of choice in clothing and are free (in principle) to purchase anything they want, in fact they are often swept up and carried along in certain ways — by fads and crazes. That's what "fashion" is all about. Fashion is, after all, a form of collective behavior and the choices that people often make frequently are decisions to go along with millions of other people in wearing some garment or adopting some style of dress that's "hot."

Many people wish to avoid standing out in the crowd, being noticed. Teenagers, who are under a great deal of pressure to conform to the "in" styles (and peer pressure is very powerful for teenagers), have to keep changing to stay the same, so to speak. For them, fashion is a coercive force which requires them to keep up with the latest trends in order to stay unnoticed or avoid being different or perceived as square or "uncool."

This affects children as well. A number of years ago I spent a year in England on sabbatical. I informed my children (my daughter was twelve and my son eight) that students in English schools wore uniforms. 'No way!' they said. The idea was just too absurd to be entertained. And yet one day after school began in London, both my children decided that since everyone else in the schools was wearing a uniform, they would also wear one. In my daughter's school, they abandoned shirts and ties for girls and my daughter wore a checkered blouse. My son wore a white shirt, tie and gray pants, and when the spring came, gray shorts. That year, I may add, there were no fights about what to wear to school. It was simply marvelous.

These school uniforms, incidentally, perform one of the more important functions of fashion — enabling people to distinguish between groups and social classes. In England you can tell what school children attend by the color of their ties and their school uniforms and this applies to us in America where we have, in selected cases, the phenomenon of the "old school tie." There is frequently a connection between the school and the socioeconomic class of the students, so the uniforms both reflect and reinforce class consciousness among the students and other members of English society.

The essence of fashion is change. But how this change comes about is problematical. In aristocratic societies, the styles were often set by the nobility and royalty and upperclasses. In democratic societies, the source of changes in fashion is not so easily located, and often styles move up from lower-class and working-class people to the upper classes and from young people to middle-aged people who are under pressure, especially in America, to look "young." In egalitarian societies, or, rather, in societies with egalitarian values, there is also a good deal of pressure on people not to appear different from others. That is why wearing blue jeans is so useful, since wearing jeans and denim clothing, a phenomenon I call "denimization," tends to mask social and class differences in people.

We also have a vast advertising industry to help generate changes in styles by creating feelings of dissatisfaction with the way we are, sartorially speaking—though the way we dress is the result of a previous dissatisfaction with the way we dressed at an earlier time. Statistics show that in America, now, young people between sixteen and nineteen spend a great deal of money each week on clothes.

In an article entitled "The Young Are Getting And Spending, Too" by Trish Hall in the 23 August 1990 edition of *The New York Times*, we find the following:

> Children often have allowances, while teen-agers take on after-school jobs. The summer is an especially lucrative time, providing teen-agers with the chance to accumulate money for what they most want—clothes. This is the leading purchase for girls and boys 16 to 19 years old consuming a third of the $73.95 a week that girls have to spend, according to the Rand Youth Poll, a market research company in New York.

The article adds that children six to fourteen "are believed to have $6 billion in discretionary income." And what these young children want to purchase are things they see advertised on television and things that their friends have. As an example, the article mentions a young thirteen-year old who "knows exactly the brands he wants to have in his wardrobe," brands such as Gotcha and Ocean Pacific.

As we grow up, watch television programs and films, look at magazines and newspapers, we make connections in our minds between certain kinds and classes of people and the clothes they wear. These metonymic associations become formalized in our

minds as "codes" and these fashion codes are part of a more gener-
alized set of rules we internalize, often called "culture codes."
What we call culture and society can be seen as collections of codes
which shape our behavior in many different areas. Socialization,
from this perspective, involves learning which codes to apply in
which social situations.

We have already seen that in England people can often, with a
fair degree of accuracy, determine the class to which a young student belongs. These codes affect fashion. For example, clothes
tend to be age-graded. We don't find it "correct" for elderly women
to wear mini-skirts and when we find an old lady who does wear
them, we tend to assume she is somewhat strange. Old women
should dress the way old women are "supposed" to dress (nonsex-
ually), though young girls can wear "granny skirts." In the same
manner middle-aged men risk ridicule if they wear clothes that are
"too young" for them, though the range is much broader here than
it is for old ladies.

These rules are connected to beliefs we have (often mistaken, I
should point out) about sexuality amongst the elderly, though,
fortunately, we are learning more about sexuality and old age and
now recognize that old people (like very young people and everyone else) are sexual beings.

Clothes are often indicators of occupation. Thus we talk about
the three-piece "business suit" and the code of dress of the busi-
nessman. Madison Avenue advertising executives were once characterized in a book as men in "gray flannel" suits. And, if I remember
correctly, pink shirts were seen as the color that went best with
these suits.

Lawyers tend to dress conservatively, as a way of stressing their
sobriety and seriousness. And the uniform of choice for professors
(at least in the public imagination) was the tweed suit, which was
typically accompanied by the bulging leather briefcase. In the
same manner, we tend to visualize doctors as wearing white coats
and carrying stethoscopes around their necks. We live in a world of
images and clothing and props (like bookcases full of law books or
medical instruments such as stethoscopes) are powerful visual indicators that help us identify people's professions.

There is an obvious relation between occupation and social class, which means that when fashion indicates people's occupations, it is indirectly indicating something about their social class. In *Radical Chic*, Tom Wolfe captured the differences in styles and taste at two ends of the socioeconomic spectrum. He describes various socialites at a party in "bell-bottom silk pants suits, Pucci clings, Gucci shoes [and] Capucci scarves." This he contrasts with the style of grape workers who were "all in work clothes, Levi's, chinos, Sears balloon-seat twills, K-Mart sports shirts, and so forth." The grape-workers style is what might be called farm worker couture and contrasts markedly with another style of clothes, the flashy dress Wolfe calls "Pimp" style. The pimp wears "the $150 Sly Stone-style vest and pants outfit from the haberdasheries on Polk [a street in San Francisco] and the $35 Lester Chambers-style four-inch-brim black beaver fedora."

It is, actually, at the extremes where fashion is most interesting for it is here that, in various ways, people call attention to themselves and create identities for themselves that are considerably different from those of the ordinary man and woman in American society. The pimp's style of dress is a sign of his occupation and, and Wolfe points out, functions as a status-symbol in the context of the streets. By middle-class standards, pimp style is loud and vulgar — but the pimp is not out to impress middle-class people.

Orrin E. Klapp makes an interesting point about fashion in his book *Collective Search for Identity*. "Fashion," he says, "is most important for those who have something to prove about themselves — especially when they cannot prove it by other means" (1962,75). He then makes some distinctions which are useful here — between *front*, *fad*, and *pose*. *Front* is a style "devoted to maintaining a social position to which one has a reasonably valid claim." Front has the function of reinforcing identity and status by placing a person in a social setting. *Fad* is experimental, frivolous and not to be taken seriously. But it is interesting, Klapp says, because it is "a more or less conscious experiment in identity (which may be engaged in by a whole peer group), which looms larger than merely maintaining position or front." Finally there is *pose*, which is a claim to an identity and social status that one is not entitled to in terms of one's status, education, and attainments.

The difficulty we find in judging people accurately by their dress stems from the problem we have in separating front from pose. As the discussion of signs in the chapter on semiotics suggested, if signs can be used to tell the truth, they can also be used to lie. (In the analysis of the clothes of secret agents, it was shown how clothes can be used to create illusions.) People, we all know, sometimes dress "above" their station and function as "impostors" with claims to status that they don't "really" deserve. Klapp mentions all kinds of poseurs: eccentrics, impostors, role vacationists, dandies, and poseurs supported by deviant groups (such as bohemians, hippies, etc.).

The different fashions or looks that some people adopt (which, in extreme form, become what Klapp labels as "ego-screaming") are symptomatic of serious dislocations in American society and exist because people are struggling to reconcile their desire for a sense of individuality and distinctiveness with the pressures to conform exerted by society.

What has happened, Klapp argues, is that fashion has become separated from its social role and has become attached to the ego. Fashions, he suggests, are now "symbols of the ego" since there has been a "shift from status symbolism to ego symbolism." The aberrations found in the styles of some people are not indications of individuality but, instead, of an anomic or antisocial stance towards things. Another way of putting this would be to say that people who dress in "extreme" ways seem to be interested, essentially, in the psychological gratifications they get from the way they dress—not that this has ever been absent from fashion.

I had an uncle who wore clothes from Brooks Brothers for fifty or sixty years. He always said he wanted to look like a person who might be the president of Princeton university, though my uncle never went to Princeton or any other university. He looked as though he had, however. He appreciated the aesthetic and sensuous quality of clothes and was very fussy about everything from his shoes to his underwear. In fact, he drove salespeople at Brooks Brothers crazy, always wanting the length of his sleeves reduced by an eighth of an inch, or his pants lengthened by some small fraction of an inch. But when he was dressed up he had a presence and a sense of satisfaction about himself that was quite obvious. We feel differently about ourselves when we wear a suit from Brooks Brothers than when we wear one from Sears and people perceive us differently, also.

Klapp discusses the changes that have occurred in the function of fashion (1962,109):

> Fashion has always advertised the person and "costumed the ego," as Edward Sapir said; but the tendency to extremes (ego-screaming) and garishness and bad taste today suggest that it is doing more along these lines and less for its traditional function of class maintenance. Fashion is ceasing to be a hallmark by which classes can distinguish themselves and more a highly theatrical adventure in identity.

Klapp wrote this in 1962; since then, I would suggest, the trend towards masking class distinctions has grown stronger. One might argue, also, that this is a good thing, that it is desirable to lessen perceived differences between people (such as the differences between social classes) and that people should not be judged on matters extraneous to their personality and character.

This notion neglects the fact that people have traditionally used dress (among other things) as a means of distinguishing between people and classes and when these differences are blurred we often get confusion. As Quentin Bell writes in *On Human Finery* (1978, 20):

> In almost any society clothes tell us the sex of the wearer and usually classify men and women into adults and children; further distinctions of class, occupation, faith and rank are common to most cultures.

The notion that there is a relationship between fashion and the social order and character is not unique to Klapp or Bell. In one of Frederick Jackson Turner's seminar essays on American character analyzing the impact of the frontier, we find the following:

> The wilderness masters the colonist. It finds him a European in dress, industries, tools, modes of travel and thought. It takes him from the railroad car and puts him in the birch canoe. It strips off the garments of civilization and arrays him in the hunting shirt and moccasin.

Before the "strangers in the land" could become Americans, they had to divest themselves of the clothes they wore, which were symbolic of their attachment to European culture and history. A new man needs new clothes, clothes that will reflect his democratic beliefs and aspirations.

The pioneer's dress was both functional in the wilderness and perfectly clear in its meaning. It symbolized people who lived in nature and innocence in contrast to our perceptions of Europeans as living in decadence and overrefinement. We wore plain clothes, of leather, while the Europeans wore fancy silks. The modern manifestation of the "plain style" found in pioneer's dress, is, of course, blue jeans—pants which are associated all over the world with American culture and society.

In *Some Fruits of Solitude* (1693) William Penn offered some words of advice about fashion:

> 73. Excess in *Apparel* is another *costly* Folly: The very Trimming of the vain World would *cloath* all the *naked* one.
> 74. Chuse the Cloaths by thine owne Eyes, not anothers. The more plain and simple they are, the better. Neither unshapely nor Fantastical; and for Use and Decency, and not for Pride.

He understood the nature of fashion very well but he underestimated the power of fashion in society. And he didn't anticipate the development of a gigantic advertising industry which seems to have convinced millions of teenage boys that life without $150 basketball sneakers (which are to be worn with the laces untied) is not worth living.

Whence the power of jeans? It is noteworthy that an article of work clothes—be it stylized, derived—should be victorious in the youth culture of initially the capitalist countries. The victory radiated, as everyone knows, far beyond the boundaries of youth culture and even deep into the socialist societies. This commodity and the cultural practices developed around it relate to bourgeois culture, narrowly defined, in a polemical way. Jeans are "leisure wear" for all employees who, at their workplace, are subjected to dress codes which prohibit blue jeans. The power of the jeans culture is attributable to its character as a complex and ever-fluctuating process of compromise between the insubordination culture and the mass culture organized by the mass media and the monopolies. Jeans, then, are multiply contended. First, between "below" and "above," and the result is a compromise between the jeans-culture-from-below and the jeans-culture-from-above. Secondly, between the heterogenous jeans interests and the economic and ideological interests of "proper" bourgeois fashion.
— Wolfgang Fritz Haug,
Commodity Aesthetics, Ideology and Culture

11

Ideological Aspects of Fashion

Fashion can not only reflect a person's ideological position (for example, the look of Skinheads) but it is also, by nature, ideological in the broadest sense of the term. The cornerstone of fashion is change and attitudes towards change are of central importance in shaping political views.

What it is that leads people to change fashions or looks is a complicated matter. Some have suggested that novelty, our seemingly innate desire for something new, different and unusual, is important here. This explanation is essentially a psychological one. There is another way of explaining fashion which is more connected to politics and ideology. From this perspective fashion is tied to alienation.

Alienation is generally interpreted to mean "lack of connection" or "sense of estrangement" from society. Literally the term "alien" means no ties or no connections. Alienated people see themselves as strangers in their own lands. For Marx, alienation is the central problem of bourgeois societies, which can provide people with goods and services but which, he argued, inevitably generates class conflict, consumer lust, and alienation — from oneself as well as from others.

In one respect — and I'm admittedly exaggerating things here — every style change people make reflects an abandonment of a previously liked "look." We become, somehow, dissatisfied with how we look and this weak form of alienation leads to the adoption of a new look which, in the future we will also discard as we move on, endlessly, from one style to another.

When one decides to dress "informally" it implies a rejection of a previous "formal" style (and one can use many other terms besides formal and informal and can think of things like hairstyles, glasses, and many other phenomena here). We have to reject, one way or another, a style that we previously found acceptable and which, itself, was built on the rejection of yet another style of dress.

Now fashion, as we have already suggested, is a social force which carries people along with it. People become alienated from their personal taste (as reflected in the style one used to dress in) in order to look fashionable, which means, in a sense, looking like many other people. Fashion is built upon a continual capacity for alienation, for if people decided that they like the way they look and don't want to accept the latest style innovation, fashion, as we know it, has lost its force.

Fashion is not based upon anomie; in fact, the existence of fashions or "looks" which become popular suggests that those who follow fashion may be alienated (from their own taste) but they are not anomic by any means. Just the opposite, in fact. I have been dealing with generalities, here, and am discussing the matter at a high level of abstraction, but the phenomena I've discussed do take place.

In my discussion of sociological aspects of fashion I suggested that sometimes fashion change comes from below, from subcultures — to which we might add, in some cases, depressed classes and ethnic minorities. But much of fashion comes from a small group of people (editors of influential magazines, superstar designers, fashion coordinators for films, etc.) whose influence is very great, even though they are not always successful in getting a certain look or style adopted. Every once in a while, for instance, women decide they don't like a certain length skirt or whatever and a style "bombs," but generally speaking, this group of fashion influentials has enormous power.

The situation is analagous to what Marx suggested takes place in society: (1964,78)

> The ideas of the ruling class are, in every age, the ruling ideas: i.e., the class which is the dominant *material* force in society is at the same time its dominant *intellectual* force. . . . The dominant ideas are nothing more than the ideal expression of the dominant material relationships, the dominant material relationships grasped as ideas. (Marx 1964,78)

If we substitute the term "fashions" for "ideas" or "designer elites" for "ruling class" we have a Marxist explanation for fashion. The dominant fashions, to transpose things a bit, and all the other dominant ideas in society are the ideas and fashions of the ruling classes, and a subelement of that are the designer elites who control society and, indirectly, fashion.

Let us explore now the matter of fashion and class.

Marx argued that capitalism created alienation and class conflict and that a revolution was needed to enable a good society to come into creation—a society in which there would be no classes and in which everyone would own (in principle, at least) the means of production. One way capitalists resisted was by "mystifying" the masses—by giving them all kinds of illusions about themselves and their possibilities which would hinder them and, even better, prevent them from organizing themselves and seizing power.

It is here that fashion plays a role, for it mystifies the masses by convincing them that they are all members of the middle class, that they are all, as the Marxists would put it, "bourgeois." Fashion gives people illusions about themselves, creates illusions in other people and ultimately gives a whole society illusions. The illusion which fashion gives in capitalist societies is that we are all, "in essence," middle class, that we have achieved a classless, all-middle class society. This notion masks the power relationships that exist in societies. There are, so the argument goes, small groups of people at the top of the middle class pyramid and various "pockets" of poverty at the bottom of the middle class pyramid, but for all practical purposes we are all middle class.

Large number of people have access to the "latest styles" (and are absorbed by their interest in these styles). These people tend to lose sight of their class origins and problems and of the class structure of society. The mass production of clothes enables all kinds of posing and impression management by various segments of society who lose sight of ideological matters and of their true situation. In addition, the very rich don't look that different from middle-class people and lower-class people. This process is sometimes known as "embourgeoisment" and refers to the illusions working class and other members of the proletariat have about themselves as "bourgeois." In these respects, then, fashion mystifies.

It is difficult to think of something which is based on choice as involving compulsion. Fashion involves, among other things, the freedom to choose and make choices; thus fashion seems to be democratic. Choice and change are implicitly antiauthoritarian, and suggest democracy rather than, for instance, totalitarianism. If anything, fashion has anarchistic implications and it is quite true that in Western democratic societies people have almost unlimited opportunity to make their own decisions about what to wear and how to live.

The matter is more complicated than it seems, however. For hidden away in the background is the matter of compulsion — which is an essential component of fashion. This matter of the "power" of fashion has been discussed by Rene Köenig in *The Restless Image: A Sociology of Fashion*. He writes, in a chapter entitled "The All-Embracing Reality of Fashion" (1973,51):

> Fashion is indeed an unacknowledged world power. Even in the great clamor of world history it guides man with a soft yet insistent voice. But again and again we feel its all-pervading presence and stare transfixed at the great public figures of the day who sometimes have themselves been carried to the top by the currents of fashion. Fashion is thus perhaps more powerful than all the other powers of the earth.

We do not notice the power of fashion because we don't understand how it works. All we recognize is the *passion* we feel to be fashionable, to wear the latest styles, to have the latest things. Is not fashion really an iron fist in a velvet glove? Is not forced choice actually compulsion masquerading as freedom?

For fashion to exist there must be change, and if these changes are to be profitable to designers and manufacturers, people must be induced to purchase clothes on the basis of their desires, not their needs. This cannot be left to chance (to the extent that it is possible to shape changes in styles and sell people on these changes, that is). Manufacturers of clothing may not be able to determine, with precision, exactly what people will like (or be taught to want) every time. But as long as people are guided by fashion, they are committed to buying something new — and eventually will.

With some commodities changes are slower and more subtle. Every once in a while a product makes a point of *not* being stylish, such as the classic Volkswagen Beetle, although it always underwent minor modifications. In some industries there is built-in obsolescence and people are forced to purchase new products as old ones wear out — or self-destruct, to put the matter more correctly.

With clothes, however, there is the need, people feel, to move with the fashions — a compulsion that people often do not recognize or think about, but whose effects they feel. For the French Marxist Henri LeFebvre, compulsion is not a strong enough word. He uses a different word, a term which we don't ordinarily associate with fashion — terror.

In his book *Everyday Life in the Modern World* he discusses advertising's role as an ideological force and the relationship that exists between fashion and society. He asks what kind of a society does fashion "take root" in:

> The unambiguous answer to this question is that it requires first (and not solely) a terrorist society. Not that fashion alone and independently causes terror to reign, but it is an integral-integrated part of terrorist societies, and it does inspire a certain kind of terror, a certainty of terror. To be or not to be fashionable is the modern version of Hamlet's problem. Fashion governs everyday life by excluding it, for everyday life cannot be fashionable and therefore is not; the demi-gods have not (or are supposed not to have) an everyday life; their life passes every day from wonder to wonder in the sphere of fashion; and yet everyday life is there, perpetually excluded. Such is the reign of terror, especially as the "fashion" phenomenon spreads to all spheres of the intellect, art, "culture". . . . This system's knack of capturing everything within reach is unimpeachable; pressure without a specific pressure-group, it influences the whole of society and its field of action interferes with and intersects different field with frontiers that are equally vague. (LeFebvre 1971, 165–66)

In this passage LeFebvre is setting up an opposition between what he calls everyday life, the quotidian, the world of commonplaces and fashion. He argues that fashion exerts an ineluctable force on people, a force which they feel and respond to (because they must) but one which they cannot "locate" as originating anyplace, which leads them to assume, mistakenly, that this force is inconsequential and that they are free.

What fashion does, LeFebvre suggests, is to destroy everyday life, the amniotic fluid, so to speak, in which we live. Fashion attacks the quotidian, generates feelings of anxiety and relative deprivation, and places people in a perpetuum mobile of discontent that renders them susceptible to manipulation by advertising agencies.

As Jules Henry has written in *Culture Against Man* (1963,70):

> In contemporary America, children must be trained to *insatiable* consumption of *impulsive* choice and *infinite* variety. These attributes, once instilled, are converted into cash by advertising directed at children. It works on the assumption that the claim that gets into the child's brain box first is most likely to stay there, and that since in contemporary America, children manage parents, the former's brain box is the antechamber to the brainbox of the latter.

It is fashion as a general force (not confined to clothes) that generates this insatiability—a term which has a faint ring of terror about it.

This notion of terror—that may seem, on the face of it, to be something of an exaggeration—explains the difficulties many people have in purchasing clothes, even when money is not a problem. Will they make the right choice? This is connected, I believe, to previously repressed morbid psychological residues that become activated as people face the dilemma of choice and feel the need to make the "correct" one. There is pressure that is exerted and felt without a locatable pressure point.

The pressure of fashion is transmitted, LeFebvre says, through advertising (he uses the French term for advertising, publicity).

> Publicity acquires the significance of ideology, the ideology of trade, and it replaces what once was philosophy, ethics, religion and aesthetics. The time is past when advertising tried to condition the consumer by mere repetition of slogans; today the more subtle forms of publicity represent a whole attitude to life: if you know how to choose you will choose this brand and no other. (LeFebvre 1971,107)

This "attitude to life" is particularly visible in fashion advertising, which tends to be based on lifestyles and functions as the equivalent of what I've described as ideologies. LeFebvre describes how television advertising tells us how to decorate our homes, tells us how to dress, tells us how to live better. And he asks, sardonically, "who can be ungrateful enough to be uneasy" about all this?

LeFebvre is uneasy because he believes that the apparent freedom people have to choose how to decorate their homes and dress masks a hidden compulsion that drives them, what he describes as "the permanent structure" of consumption. Since it is fashion (in the broadest sense of the term) that creates "imaginary appetites" and exploits anything and everything in its ceaseless movement, it is fashion that must be scrutinized and explained. Once we accept fashion's premises and postulates (such as that one "must be stylish") we become prisoners of an all-embracing, ubiquitous, relentless system of pressure "without pressure points we can locate" that shapes our entire lives. This covers everything from furniture to automobiles to "trophy wives."

The world is simply ridiculous if one looks at it from the technical point of view. It is unpractical in all that concerns the relations between human beings, and in the highest degree uneconomical and inexact in its methods. And anyone who is in the habit of dealing with his affairs by means of a slide-rule finds that a good half of all human assertions simply cannot be taken seriously. A slide-rule consists of two incredibly ingeniously combined systems of figures and divisions; a slide-rule consists of two little white-enameled rods, the cross section of which is a flat trapezium, which slide into each other, a device by the aid of which one can instantly solve the most complicated problems, without wasting any thought on the matter; a slide-rule is a little symbol that one carries in one's breast-pocket, feeling it as a hard white line over one's heart. If one owns a slide-rule, and someone comes along with large assertions or grand feelings, one says: "just a moment, please—first of all let's work out the margin of error and the approximate value of the thing!"

—Robert Musil,
The Man Without Qualities

Conclusion
The Ghost in the Machine

This book has two dimensions to it. First, it is about material culture and what it reflects about society. In one sense, *Reading Matter* should be looked upon as a contribution to the study of everyday life, primarily in the United States — a subject that has occupied my attention for many years. I have long been interested in the mass media and popular culture and, by definition, therefore, I am a student of everyday life. And that is because the mass media and popular culture are, to a considerable degree, the contents of our lives — or, at least, of much of our leisure.

Reading Matter is, second, a methods book that suggests how different disciplines can be used to interpret material culture. The subtitle makes this point. There is, I would argue, no one way to interpret material culture, no "royal road" to understanding it and making sense of the role it plays in our lives and in society. I have used a number of different disciplines to interpret material culture and this book can be looked upon as an example of how multi-disciplinary investigations might be conducted. I have also focused on how different disciplines illuminate one topic (blue jeans, what

131

I've called "denimization," and fashion, in general) in the second half of the book.

I have suggested that as far as the academic world is concerned, we all tend to see the universe as revolving around our own disciplines. Others have made the same argument. Like the neurologist who sees all medicine as subdisciplines of neurology, scholars (all too often, I would argue) see other disciplines as subdisciplines of *their* discipline (at best). And they reserve most scorn for those who attempt interdisciplinary, crossdisciplinary, or multidisciplinary approaches to subjects of investigation.

Let me offer a personal anecdote that is relevant. I was at a conference in England a number of years ago and was talking to a British professor about my work on popular culture. I mentioned that it might be described as multidisciplinary. "Here in Britain," he said, "we call it 'undisciplinary.'" And much multidisciplinary research is undisciplined (whatever that might mean) and superficial. But so is much unidisciplinary work.

Ironically, what we often discover, I believe, is that the people who are the most profound exponents of a particular discipline end up being, sub rosa, multidisciplinary. And that is because life doesn't always arrange itself neatly enough so that one or another discipline is adequate to do justice to the complexity of things.

I have started this book with a basic premise: that material culture, understood here as the artifacts (relatively simple objects showing human workmanship) that play so large a role in our lives, both reflect our values and beliefs and affect our lives. I don't think too many people would find this notion difficult to entertain as a working hypothesis. The question is, how does one make sense of material culture? What objects and artifacts does one study? What technique or techniques are most appropriate for specific items? And, of particular importance, how do you use the methodologies (or disciplines)? I would hope that *Reading Matter* answers these questions, or, at least, suggests directions in which analysts of material culture might move.

This book is a qualitative analysis of material culture and should be looked upon as such. What I have tried to do is move from the level of discipline to that of concept and show how particular concepts, within disciplines, can be used to interpret specific objects and artifacts. Since I believe that these objects have to be seen as part of some system, in a number of cases I have suggested that a given object must be understood and interpreted as it relates to other objects and artifacts.

I believe that objects relate to one another much the same way words and concepts do — a notion that is derived from Saussure's pioneering work in linguistics. Artifacts and objects, if you will, form something very much like a language, which is one reason I used the term "reading" in my title. And frequently, as the Malinowski study of the *kula* demonstrated, while the objects themselves may be "worthless" or of little economic value, they often have enormous symbolic significance. And they frequently generate extremely important rituals and institutions, which, in turn, impact upon the lives of large numbers of people.

This notion, that we can apply a number of different approaches to interpreting material culture, assumes that these objects we study have many meanings and that different people can "read" a given object in a number of different ways. Words are often ambiguous and artifacts are multi-faceted and can be interpreted from a number of perspectives. My little story about the scholars looking at the McDonald's hamburger from their offices is not too far removed from the well-known poem about the blind men and the elephant. Each of the blind men, touching a different part of the elephant, comes to different conclusions about what elephants are like. And all, of course, are wrong. Wrong, in the sense that they overgeneralize from their limited experience (something I have been accused of doing at times, but mainly, rest assured, in my youth).

Some reader response theorists even go so far as to argue that texts (novels, plays, etc.) don't exist as things in themselves but only as they are "read" by readers, each of whom, in a sense, calls the work into creation and participates in the creation of the work. I find this notion somewhat extreme, but it does point out something that we have long neglected, namely the role people (readers, audiences, users of artifacts) play in the total scheme of things. At one time readers were seen as playing no role at all; now, for some reader response theorists, readers seem to be more important than authors.

Objects are our texts and as in all texts, the meaning is not evident; it has to be elicited from the object by a "reader" who has some way of interpreting what the object means. (For many, the meaning is the use.) We Americans may hold that certain truths are "self-evident" (a subject of considerable dispute among political scientists and philosophers) but meaning, let me suggest, is never self-evident. And what you see depends on the "goggles" (discipline, methodology, approach) you are wearing when you examine and try to interpret an object.

In this book I have drawn on the work of many different scholars representing a number of points of view. I have used work by historians, psychiatrists, Freudians, Marxists, semioticians, sociologists, anthropologists, and representatives of various other disciplines. It turns out that many people have written about material culture—whether it be cigarette lighters, Barbie Dolls, bikinis, deoderants, blue jeans, hamburgers, soup, or soap. And I have cited them all through the book. I have also offered a number of my own interpretations of artifacts—interpretations that (at times) some readers might consider a bit forced or perhaps even absurd.

It may be helpful to think of me as a whimsical sociologist, using the term in the broadest sense. Some people, perhaps many people, find my Freudian interpretations to be ridiculous, in part because they find *any* Freudian analyses to be ridiculous. Freud, as the referee of the manuscript of this book suggested, does not have a good reputation in the academy and has largely been supplanted.

I recognize this but I seem to have this compulsion, in certain instances, to use Freudian notions since they seem to explain things better than any other approaches I know of. And some of the Freudian interpretations come from others whom I've quoted. Not everyone, it turns out, rejects Freud or, perhaps more accurately, Freudian and neo-Freudian notions. The story about the woman who turned her living room into something like a bathroom (because of her allegedly unconscious problems) was not invented by me, remember, but was from a work by a respected psychiatrist.

My neurologist hiking partner considers Freudian ideas to be not just nonsense but "complete nonsense." He keeps plugging for what he calls a "bio-psycho-social" approach, and yet I find that in our conversations every so often he is "guilty" of falling back on

Freudian notions. In part, I suggest, because they are so much part of our lives and thought processes. But also, let me suggest, because he can't find a better explanation of things.

This is not the place to "resolve" the matter of the validity of Freudianism. There may be, perhaps, no way to resolve this matter. For years Freudianism was extremely popular (and it still is in certain fields, such as literary criticism and literary theory) and widely accepted. Now it is no longer in favor and widely scorned and abused. Let me suggest that you consider whether or not my use of Freudian concepts, found, I might add, only here and there in the book, helps make sense of things, has the possibility of being correct, has some kind of "face value" reasonability — and leave the issue there. But there is another methodology that needs discussion here — Marxism.

There is, currently, a major debate among scholars about the status of Marxism. *Reading Matter* is not a Marxist book, but it does make use of Marxist concepts at times, and deals, in particular, with the work of Wolfgang Haug. He commits the additional sin of using Freudian notions in his work. The question we have to consider here is this — is Marxism dead? (A book by Jean-Marie Benoist, published a number of years ago in France, says "Yes.")

The various totalitarian Communist regimes in Eastern Europe and Russia, itself, have lost legitimacy and are now thoroughly discredited. At one time the Marxist societies could argue, at least, that they were morally superior to capitalist ones. We now have discovered, thanks to the revolutions in Romania and elsewhere, that this was just a big charade. Does Marxism, which provided the philosophical rationale for communism, also deserve a place on the junk heap (a place dear to the heart of analysts of material culture) of history?

We must keep this question in mind, at least, when we look at how Marxist concepts can help us make sense of our material culture. I would argue that American Marxists (we seem to be the only country where Marxist thought is still flourishing) have not dreamed of establishing Socialism, let alone Communism, in America. Instead, they have used Marx's ideas as a means of critiquing or attacking many of the abuses they find (or believe exist, which is not the same thing) in American society.

Perhaps they are best understood, using Wildavsky's typology, as Egalitarians, whose mission in life it is to criticize both the Elitists and the Competitive Individualists and "help raise" up what Wildavsky calls the Fatalists. Here, too, I would argue, we have to see whether the Marxist perspective helps us, literally, make sense of things. If any of Marx's concepts seem reasonable and offer insights about our material culture and society, I suggest we use them.

It may be that systems of thought such as Freudianism and Marxism are not "disproved" as much as "abandoned." What really happens is that we become bored with them and find ourselves attracted by other approaches. It may be, also, that when we start examining methodologies and disciplines closely, we find all kinds of problems with them.

Whatever the case, I have used Freudian and Marxist thought (or, more precisely, concepts from them) as methods of interpretation and leave the matter of deciding whether these systems are useful or correct (or both) to the reader. One more "role" for the reader. Some people have described my work as dealing with that which is obvious to everyone. "Everyone knows this," they say. Others argue that my work (or some of it) is farfetched and ridiculous. I am accused of being "feverishly" inventive, with no concern for what is reasonable, demonstrable, provable or nonprovable. (I do confess to never having rejected a null hypothesis). I argue that my work, whatever its limitations, cannot be both common knowledge and obvious to everyone and, at the same time, far out and ridiculous.

I hope that *Reading Matter* might lead my readers to investigate material culture themselves. The world is full of seemingly ordinary things that are, when you start looking at them carefully, really quite interesting and remarkable. The world is full of things that "cry out" for interpretation. If those who hear or read your interpretations "cry out," I would take it as a sign that you have somehow touched a very sensitive nerve and are on the right track.

If, at some moment, as you are about the press a button on some appliance or other device, or find yourself looking longingly at an advertisement for some gismo, you pause for a moment and think about what it all means or might mean, *Reading Matter* will have served its purpose.

References

Barthes, Roland. 1970. *Writing Degree Zero and Elements of Semiology*. Boston: Beacon Press.

Barthes, Roland. 1972. *Mythologies*. New York: Hill & Wang.

Barthes, Roland. 1982. *Empire of Signs*. New York: Hill & Wang.

Berger, Arthur Asa. 1974. *About Man: An Introduction to Anthropology*. Dayton, OH: Pflaum/Standard.

Berger, Arthur Asa. 1982. *Media Analysis Techniques.* Newbury Park, CA: SAGE Publications.

Berger, Arthur Asa. 1989. *Signs In Contemporary Culture: An Introduction to Semiotics*. New York: Annenberg-Longman.

Braudel, Fernand. 1981. *The Structures of Everyday Life: The Limits of the Possible*. New York: Harper and Row.

Brenner, Charles. 1974. *An Elementary Textbook of Psychoanalysis*. New York: Doubleday Anchor Books.

Briggs, Asa. 1988. *Victorian Things*. London: B. T. Botsford.

Culler, Jonathan. 1976. *Structuralist Poetics: Structuralism, Linguistics and the Study of Literature*. Ithaca, NY: Cornell University Press.

Dichter, Ernest. 1960. *The Strategy of Desire*. London: Boardman.

Dichter, Ernest. 1964. *Handbook of Consumer Motivations: The Psychology of the World of Objects*. New York: McGraw-Hill.

Eco, Umberto. 1967. *A Theory of Semiotics*. Bloomington, IN: Indiana University Press.

Eliade, Mircea. 1959. *The Sacred and The Profane*. New York: Harvest Books.

Fairchild, Henry Pratt. 1967. *Dictionary of Sociology and Related Sciences*. Totawa, NY: Littlefield, Adams & Co.

Fishwick, Marshall and Ray B. Browne. 1970. *Icons of Popular Culture*. Bowling Green, OH: Bowling Green University Popular Press.

Foerster, Norman. 1957. *American Poetry and Prose: Fourth Edition, Volume One*. Boston: Houghton Mifflin.

Forty, Adrian. 1986. *Objects of Desire: Design and Society from Wedgwood to IBM*. New York: Pantheon.

Freud, Sigmund. 1953. *A General Introduction to Psychoanalysis*. New York: Permabooks.

Freud, Sigmund. 1963. *Character and Culture*. New York: Collier Books.

Freud, Sigmund. 1965. *The Interpretation of Dreams*. New York: Avon Books.

Goffman, Erving. 1969. *Strategic Interaction*. Philadelphia, PA: University of Pennsylvania Press.

Goffman, Erving. 1971. *Relations in Public*. New York: Harper Colophon.

Gowans, Alan. 1981. *Learning to See*. Bowling Green, OH: Bowling Green University Popular Press.

Grotjahn, Martin. 1966. *Beyond Laughter: Humor and the Subconscious*. New York: McGraw-Hill.

Harris, Marvin. 1974. *Cows, Pigs, Wars and Witches*. New York: Vintage Books.

Haug, Wolfgang Fritz. 1986. *Critique of Commodity Aesthetics: Appearance, Sexuality and Advertising in Capitalist Society*. Minneapolis, MN: University of Minnesota Press.

Huizinga, Johan. 1924. *Waning of the Middle Ages*. New York: Doubleday Anchor Books.

Klapp, Orrin E. 1969. *Collective Search for Identity*. New York: Holt, Rinehart and Winston.

Kron, Joan. July, 26, 1990. *New York Times*.

Lavers, Annette. 1982. *Roland Barthes: Structuralism and After*. Cambridge, MA: Harvard University Press.

Leach, Edmund. 1976. *Culture and Communications: The Logic by Which Symbols are Connected*. Cambridge: Cambridge University Press.

LeFebvre, Henri. 1984. *Everyday Life in the Modern World*. New Brunswick, NJ: Transaction Books.

MacCannell, D. 1976. *The Tourist: A New Theory of the Leisure Class*. New York: Schocken Books.

Malinowski, Bronislaw. 1922. *Argonauts of the Western Pacific*. New York: Dutton.

Marx, Karl. 1964. *Selected Writings in Sociology and Social Philosophy*. T. Bottomore and M. Ruvol, eds. New York: McGraw-Hill.

McLuhan, Marshall. 1967. *The Mechanical Bride*. Boston, MA: Beacon Press.

Meiselman, Moshe. "Clothing our bodies—discerning the holy." *Sh/ma: A Journal of Jewish responsibility*. Nov. 14, 1976.

Patai, Raphael. 1972. *Myth and Modern Man*. Englewood Cliffs, NJ: Prentice-Hall.

Sapirstein, Milton R. 1955. *Paradoxes of Everyday Life*. New York: Premier.

Saussure, Ferdinand de. 1966. *A Course in General Linguistics*. New York: McGraw-Hill.

Sebeok, Thomas. (Ed.) 1977. *A Perfusion of Signs*. Bloomington, IN: Indiana University Press.

Turner, Victor. 1974. *Dramas, Fields, and Metaphors: Symbolic Action in Human Society*. Ithaca, NY: Cornell University Press.

Warner, W. Lloyd. 1963. *Yankee City*. New Haven, CN: Yale University Press.

Winick, Charles. 1968. *The New Poeple: Desexualization in American Life*. New York: Pegasus.

Name Index

Subject Index